MURDER IN THE COURTHOUSE

MURDER IN THE COURTHOUSE

RECONSTRUCTION & REDEMPTION IN THE NORTH CAROLINA PIEDMONT

JIM WISE

THE History PRESS

Published by The History Press
Charleston, SC 29403
www.historypress.net

Front cover images: William Woods Holden as a young man. *Courtesy North Carolina State Archives.*
Caswell County Courthouse, where John W. Stephens was murdered. *Author's photo.*
Back cover images: Magazine illustrations of political participation by African Americans under Reconstruction. *Courtesy North Carolina State Archives.*

First published 2010

Manufactured in the United States

ISBN 978.1.59629.755.5

Library of Congress Cataloging-in-Publication Data

Wise, James E., 1949-
Murder in the courthouse : Reconstruction and redemption in the North Carolina Piedmont / Jim Wise.
p. cm.
Includes bibliographical references.
ISBN 978-1-59629-755-5
1. North Carolina--History--1865- 2. North Carolina--Politics and government--1865-1950. 3. Reconstruction (U.S. history, 1865-1877)--North Carolina. 4. Martial law--North Carolina--History--19th century. 5. Holden, W. W. (William Woods), 1818-1892. 6. Stephens, John Walter, 1834-1870. 7. Murder--North Carolina--Yanceyville.
I. Title.
F259.W65 2010
975.6'04--dc22
2009050440

For Joe Huber
A teacher and a good man

CONTENTS

AUTHOR'S NOTE

I'll credit, or blame, two people for inspiring me to write this book. First, my friend Jack Schrader, who several years ago asked me to speak to our local Civil War Roundtable on Reconstruction in our area—that being Durham County, North Carolina. I didn't find much to go on, just some general treatments about the whole state in the early post–Civil War period and a newspaper clip about the adventures of two local men in the Reconstruction Ku Klux Klan. But the period had brought Durham's foundation as a tobacco-manufacturing hub—part of an industrializing trend in North Carolina begun before the war and accelerating afterward. So with that story to fill some time, the talk went off okay.

The second individual is my cousin Mike Martinez, whose excellent and pleasantly readable *Carpetbaggers, Cavalry and the Ku Klux Klan*, about the Reconstruction Klan in South Carolina and the U.S. officer who was largely responsible for breaking it, piqued my curiosity about the period in North Carolina again. Reading Mike's book brought to mind a vague memory about some incident up in Caswell County—something about somebody shot (so I remembered it) in the courthouse and somebody called "Chicken." So motivated, I looked up the incident and realized there was a story to be told.

In preparing myself to tell it, I was immensely aided by the good folks of the Caswell County Historical Association, who maintain a marvelously stocked museum just off the square in Yanceyville and one of the richest local history web presences I've ever come across. Rick Frederick was generous with information and advice and graciously gave permission to reproduce images from the association's excellent collection.

I am also indebted to Kim Cumber, of the North Carolina State Archives, for assistance in locating images from its collection and for expedited processing of my request for copies.

Many other people's aid over the years went into the foundation upon which *Murder in the Courthouse* is built. My particular appreciation goes to the Durham County Public Library for its wealth of printed resources, and to the University of North Carolina for its rich repository of the state's history and the elegant reading room in which a researcher may use it.

And, as always, gratitude and love to my wife, Babs, for her support and patience.

MAY 21, 1870

The Victim

Whatever were they thinking?

What was going through your mind, Chicken Stephens, when you were facing your last moments in the presence of your enemies? Anger? Fear? Regret? All your precautions, all your arms, undone by one little, inexplicable lapse of judgment. Do you, just for one instant, question the rightness of what you did, who you were? Just an instant—as you felt the rope around your neck, the knife across your throat?

John Walter, aka "Chicken," Stephens really should have known better.

Radical Republican, known spy for the scalawag governor, suspected of barn burning and murder, widely considered to have stolen his seat in the North Carolina Senate from a duly elected local hero—he brazenly walked into the Democrats' convention at the Caswell County Courthouse, brashly sat down in the front row and blithely went about taking notes.

It was Saturday, chilly for so late in the spring, but in the Caswell County seat of Yanceyville it was a busy day. Country folk in town to shop and hang around, teamsters hauling tobacco stopping off at the public well, property owners at the courthouse to declare their taxes and three hundred Democrats—or Conservatives, as the party was also known at the time—come to plan for the state elections in August.

That meant at least three hundred men who had no use for John Walter Stephens.

Being a state official of the ruling Republican Party, and an agent for the governor, Stephens was a powerful man in Caswell County, but his power was matched by his unpopularity. His fellow Methodists had even kicked him out of their congregation for his activities with the Union League—a secretive society that organized former slaves into a Republican political bloc and conducted other, fiery and violent, maneuvers under cover of night.

Freed African Americans were the Republicans' base in North Carolina, which was itself, thus, a base of support for the Republicans in Washington who had forced Congressional Reconstruction down former Confederate throats. As such, freedmen and their white handlers and allies were targets for Conservatives in the legislature, at the ballot box and through other, fiery and violent, maneuvers under cover of night by that other secretive society: the Ku Klux Klan.

As targets go, "Chicken" Stephens—so called from a violent episode over a neighbor's fowl—would be a Kluxer prize.

Indications are that he knew it. He had heard threats, and his wife, Martha, had seen strange men loitering outside their house for several nights. Earlier that year, Stephens had bought a $10,000 life-insurance policy, written his will and fortified the house, and he now slept inside an iron cage with a veritable arsenal of firearms near to hand. When he went out, he carried two derringers and a Colt revolver.

Still, he went to hear what the Conservatives would have to say.

What was on his mind? Later, his wife would say that he had eaten none of his midday dinner, claiming he felt unwell, and on the street that morning some stranger yelled at him to "Shoo!" She tried to talk him out of going to the meeting, but he said he must and left the house. On the way to the courthouse, his niece stopped Stephens in the street and warned him that there would be trouble. "I am not going to bother anyone and one had better not bother me," he said—or words to that effect.

Once at the courthouse, Stephens went to take care of his taxes, parried an assessor's questions about his stock of weapons and then stopped to talk to Frank Wiley. Wiley had been county sheriff, and Stephens wanted him to run again—but as a Republican. Wiley said he'd give Stephens his decision later that afternoon.

Stephens walked up the spiral staircase to the courtroom, an ornate testimony to the county's prosperity with its cast-iron railings, decorative Corinthian columns and ribbed ceiling. The orators orated and a couple of hours passed, and Stephens got a message that Wiley wanted to talk.

Stephens left the courtroom and met Wiley, and the two went downstairs to a small storeroom at the back of the courthouse that was quiet and out of the way. They went inside, and three other men appeared as Wiley left and closed the door.[1]

A subsequent biographer wondered:

> *It is a matter of wonder and astonishment to those who know him well, his habits, his fears and his exceedingly great caution, that he should have gone into an unoccupied room and suffered the door locked and double bolted with any person or persons, whom he did not* believe *were at least to be his personal and political friends.*[2]

Stephens had told his wife he'd be home at five o'clock for supper.

He didn't make it.

The Governor

And you, Governor William Woods Holden, what did you have on the brain that chilly May afternoon? For certain, you had much to dwell upon. Your party's splits and power plays? The state's $30 million debt with its bonds selling for three cents on the dollar? The railroad scandals the opposition was pinning on your administration even though the opposition feasted at the trough itself? Perhaps your duty as a governor, with civil wars going on in one county after another?

It being a Saturday, Holden might have been enjoying his flowers. It being May, the sunken garden behind his Raleigh home would have been at its springtime finest. The state's official governor's residence was still a wreck from the visit of General W.T. Sherman's Union army four years earlier, and Holden had simply remained in his own residence at Hargett and McDowell Streets, an easy two-block walk from the stately Capitol.

The governor styled himself, and likely thought of himself, as a champion of the common man,[3] but the home he had built in 1852 reflected his stature as one of the state's elite. It was a wood-framed square with four interior chimneys, a two-story Classical portico on the front and first-floor porches on either side where Holden paced, wrote, played with his children and did some of his thinking.[4]

Inside, there was carved mahogany furniture, a spiral staircase and one of Raleigh's first indoor bathtubs. Outside, there was the garden of flowers, boxwood shrubs and trees, including the only weeping elm in town. It was a spacious, convivial place, and the Holdens—he, risen from the toiling classes, and she, the former Louisa Virginia Harrison, daughter of a prominent Raleigh businessman and politician and a second cousin of the late U.S. president William Henry Harrison—were known for their hospitality and entertainments.

At this time, though, the governor was better known for statehouse corruption, crippled finances in a state unrecovered from the Recent Unpleasantness and his alliances with carpetbaggers, opportunists and Republicans—the fourth political party to which Holden had given his time, talent and sometimes-questioned loyalties. A one-time admirer of the South Carolina firebrand John C. Calhoun, a champion of states' rights and an owner of slaves, Holden had also called for peace talks while Robert E. Lee was still winning, allied himself with the floundering postwar policies of Raleigh native Andrew Johnson and now was a champion of Negro suffrage.

Holden might, that afternoon, even have been thinking about Caswell County, and about this man Stephens, who was making himself a problem. In some counties, Holden had been able to stem Ku Klux violence by enlisting the aid of prominent and cool-headed Conservatives. He tried the same in Caswell, but the man he had contacted there, Thomas A. Donoho, had just written the governor: "It is an unfortunate circumstance for the welfare of the county, as well as for the interest of your party, that the recognized exponent of the Republican party in the county, should be a person of the antecedents and surroundings of the member who represents the county in the State Senate."[5]

What was a governor to do?

Holden was going to make history. Just not the history he would have liked.

THE PERP

And you, John G. Lea, what was in your mind there in that small back room of the courthouse with the man you have condemned facing you and asking for his life? What do you see—chicken thief, murderer, traitor? Political hack, spy for that man in Raleigh who was crying "Peace" at the same time you were riding with General Lee!? Nigger lover? All of the above?

John G. Lea might have been wondering what he had for men. Here they had Chicken Stephens right where they wanted him: disarmed, alone, helpless.

His Caswell Kluxers had given Stephens a fair trial—the defendant had not been invited, however—found him guilty and sentenced him to die. Today was the date agreed upon, and here he was. So wasn't somebody going to go on and get it over with?

Wiley had ducked out as soon as Stephens was delivered. James Mitchell, James Denny and Joe Fowler had been waiting, as planned. Mitchell took Stephens's guns away and then went away himself and left Denny, pistol at Stephens's head, to do the honors. After a minute or two, Denny left and told Wiley that he just couldn't go through with it.

Now, afraid of being found out, Wiley found Lea in conversation with some other convention-goers and told Lea he'd better do something. Lea and the other men rushed to the storeroom, where Stephens was sitting on the floor. When Stephens saw Lea, he stood and came up to him. The two men sat together on a pile of firewood, and Stephens asked Lea to protect him.

Mitchell by now was back with a rope noose, and at this point he rushed at Stephens, whipped the noose around his neck and pulled it tight. Half a dozen others ran up, among them Lea's fellow Confederate veteran Tom Oliver. Oliver had a pocketknife out, and he rammed it into Stephens's chest, then into his throat, twice—once on each side of his Adam's apple.

They left Stephens lying there on the woodpile, the rope around his neck and the knife on the floor at his feet. The body wasn't found until the next morning, and the coroner's court of inquest concluded that Stephens's fatal wounds were "done by the hands of some unknown person, or persons, to us."[6]

The hands remained unknown—legally—for sixty-five years, but the effects came quickly and must have exceeded John G. Lea's greatest expectations.

OMINOUS VICTORY

April 17, 1865: Riding his train back to Raleigh that Tuesday evening, Major General William Tecumseh Sherman had every reason to feel satisfaction with a job well done.

In just over two and a half months, he had marched his army of eighty thousand men across five hundred miles of enemy territory. They had overcome swamps, rivers, hills, rain and any other annoying obstacles along the way and showed the Carolinas just what war was all about. They had sacked Columbia, capital of South Carolina, that "hell-hole of secession"; they had demolished the Rebel arsenal at Fayetteville; they had rolled over a Rebel army sent to stop them and occupied North Carolina's capital city with only one case of token resistance.[7]

Sherman's own opponent, Confederate general Joseph Eggleston Johnston, had favorably compared Sherman's March to the campaigns of Julius Caesar. And now, on this day, Johnston and Sherman had put an end to the War of the Rebellion and secured the basis of a peace that could last.

Or so he had every reason to believe.

With Lee having surrendered his twenty-eight-thousand-man Army of Northern Virginia on April 9, 1865, Sherman had occupied Raleigh on Thursday, April 13. It only remained for him to crush the remnants of Johnston's army, or force its surrender—that would end the war in the East, leaving only small Rebel commands in the field farther west. Over the weekend, Johnston had asked for a meeting to discuss a cessation of hostilities. They met, at a farm between Durham's Station and Hillsborough,

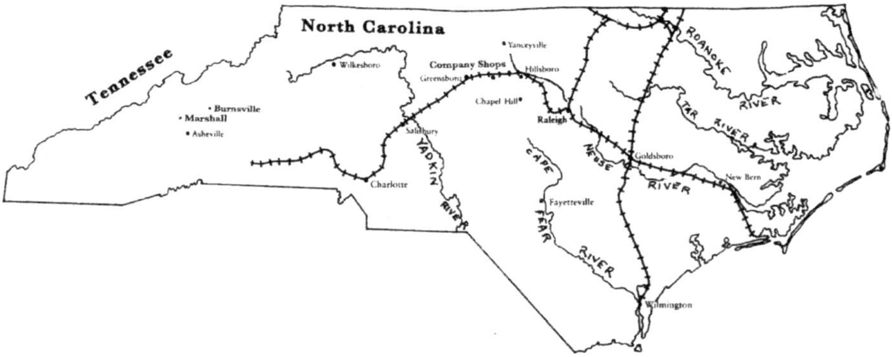

North Carolina, with major antebellum railroad lines. The Reconstruction Klan was active around Company Shops and Yanceyville. *Author's sketch.*

on Monday morning and again on Tuesday, and from the second meeting Sherman came away with a signed surrender in hand.

He would be a hero.

Arriving in Raleigh, the general went to his headquarters in the Governor's Palace on Fayetteville Street and wrote his superior, Lieutenant General Ulysses S. Grant:

> *I inclose herewith a copy of an agreement made this day between General Joseph E. Johnston and myself, which, if approved by the President of the United States, will produce peace from the Potomac* [to] *the Rio Grande… I urge, on the part of the President, speedy action, as it is important to get the Confederate armies to their homes as well as our own.*[8]

The agreement specified:

- Confederate armies to disband and turn their weapons in to their state arsenals;
- The United States government to recognize existing state governments in the former Confederacy;
- Federal courts to be reestablished in those states;
- Citizens of those states to be guaranteed their political, civil and property rights;
- The United States government "not to disturb any of the people by reason of the late war so long as they live in peace and quiet;
- A general amnesty.

Sherman sent the same letter to Major General Henry Halleck, Union commander in Virginia, with a separate note concluding: "Influence [the president] not to vary the terms at all, for I have thought of everything and believe that the Confederate Armies once dispersed, we can adjust all else fairly and well." To his wife, Ellen, he wrote, "I can hardly realize it, but I can see no slip. The terms are all on our side."[9]

Sherman and Johnston, though, had no legal authority to end the war, and until their respective presidents signed off on the terms they remained just ink on paper. But Sherman had in mind the similarly lenient terms that Grant and Lee had signed at Appomattox, and to which President Abraham Lincoln had agreed. Sherman thought he was carrying out what Lincoln had said he wanted at their meeting in Virginia on March 27 and 28.

> *He distinctly authorized me to assure Governor Vance and the people of North Carolina that, as soon as the rebel armies laid down their arms, and resumed their civil pursuits, they would at once be guaranteed all their rights as citizens of a common country; and that to avoid anarchy the State governments then in existence, with their civil functionaries, would be recognized by him as the government de facto till Congress could provide others...His earnest desire seemed to be to end the war speedily, without more bloodshed or devastation, and to restore all the men of both sections to their homes.*[10]

The Northern press praised Lincoln for his wisdom in going easy on the South,[11] but things in Washington had changed. While Sherman and Johnston were talking in North Carolina, Abraham Lincoln's body was lying in state at the White House. Andrew Johnson, a Unionist Democrat from Tennessee who was born in Raleigh, was president now. And the radical Republicans Lincoln was able to keep in check now had no such interference in their way of wreaking revenge on the South while overturning its established social order. Sherman's peace would not have the reception he expected. But the general wouldn't know that for some days yet, and in the meantime, he went about restoring law and order as best he could.

Law and order needed a lot of restoring. Apart from its tidewater region, combat remained outside the state until the war's last weeks, but civil order was breaking down even before Union troops came over the South Carolina line. Civil authority had come into conflict with military as early as 1862, particularly over conscription, giving critics of the Confederate government—notable among them, *North Carolina Standard* owner William

Woods Holden—more ammunition for their campaign to brand President Jefferson Davis a despot trampling on the very liberties that Southerners were fighting to protect.[12] As Southern defeat appeared more and more certain, Confederate deserters turned outlaw across central North Carolina, raiding and vandalizing as they pleased, with most of the able-bodied male population away in the army and little that county sheriffs and town constables could do to stop them.[13]

In Raleigh, Sherman had feared that his troops would riot when informed of Lincoln's murder, but his officers kept behavior in check and tried to stop soldiers from confiscating provisions from citizens who were already destitute. Cornelia Phillips Spencer, of the nearby university town of Chapel Hill, described the 1865 homefront: "Where many families of the highest respectability and refinement lived for months on corn-bread, sorghum, and peas…children went barefoot through the winter, and ladies made their own shoes, and wove their own homespuns; where the carpets were cut up into blankets, and window-curtains and sheets were torn up for hospital uses."[14]

Still, foraging went on—in one form or another.

> *The situation seemed to veterans to warrant the adoption of extraordinary and perhaps even questionable measures. A squad of men from the regiment went out about ten miles to a wealthy planter's and persuaded him to sell them a wagon-load of miscellaneous provisions,* very cheap. *He was permitted to accompany them to camp in order to convey the purchase with his own team and wagon, but was mildly enjoined to reply promptly to any inquirers who might ask impertinent questions about his load, that the soldiers had satisfactorily paid for it.*[15]

On April 20, Holden wrote in his newspaper:

> *Our people are just emerging from a desolating war, and a large majority of them are destitute not only of the comforts but of the necessaries of life. They have been compelled to drink the cup of "peaceabel secession" to the dregs. They have lost life, property, comforts, everything but honor; and at one time many of them feared that even hope was gone. The contest is now virtually at an end, and it is the duty of every good citizen to strengthen the arm of just authority, and to aid in bringing order from chaos, so that industry may be protected and rewarded and our former prosperity and happiness restored.*[16]

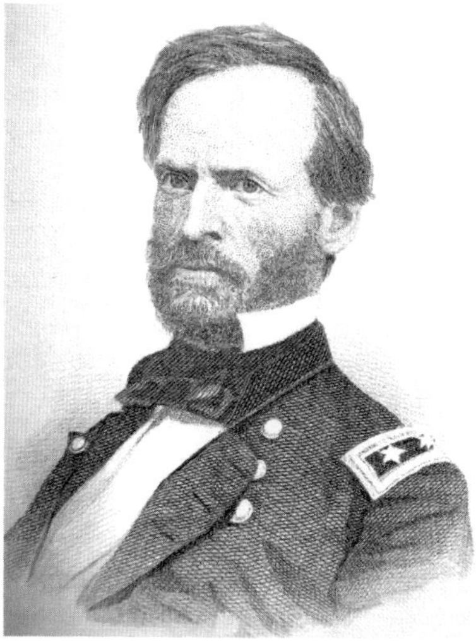

General William T. Sherman warned Union leaders against a harsh approach to the defeated South. *From Joseph Johnston's* Narrative of Military Operations.

On the run farther west in North Carolina, Jefferson Davis agreed to the Sherman-Johnston terms on April 23. However, the next morning in Raleigh, Sherman received a surprise visit from U.S. Grant. "Cump" Sherman's boss and personal friend had made the trip to break the news in person: no way was the United States going to let the Rebels off so light.

Washington was rife with rumors and conspiracy theories on the Lincoln murder, most of them implicating Confederate agents if not the Confederate government and Jefferson Davis himself. One individual of that mind was Secretary of War Edwin M. Stanton, a Unionist Democrat from Ohio who had already drawn up a plan for splitting the South into military districts in place of state governments. The new president, Johnson, was a Jacksonian Democrat from Tennessee who championed "honest yeomen," considered the planter class a "bloated, corrupted aristocracy" and antagonized his party's secessionist wing by taking a pro-Union stance even though he had been a defender of states' rights.[17] He was the only Southern senator to stay on the job in Washington after war broke out and, aligning himself with Republicans and pro-Union, pro-war Democrats, returned to Tennessee in 1864 as military governor of that part of his state under Union control. Stanton and Johnson sent Grant to Raleigh with terms of their own for the Confederate commander: give up or else.

The new conditions required a loyalty oath from Confederate soldiers; officers were allowed to keep their sidearms, horses and baggage; and the men were allowed to go home. There was nothing about recognizing state governments, nothing about setting up federal courts, nothing about a general amnesty and nothing about political, civil or property rights—the latter of which, Stanton said, could be interpreted to let Southerners keep their slaves.[18] While Grant was en route, before he could break the news to Sherman, Stanton went public with a fantastic story based on misinterpretations and rumor—to the effect that Sherman had deliberately violated an order Lincoln gave Grant in March—that he have no talks with Southerners on politics—and, further, strongly hinted that Sherman was taking a bribe to let Jefferson Davis escape, that his terms would protect slavery and that he had all but "relieved the Rebels in every degree, who had slaughtered our people, from all pains and penalties for their crimes."[19]

Meanwhile, Lincoln's funeral train was making its roundabout way from Washington to Springfield, Illinois. Emotions were raw, nerves were tight and the Northern press picked up Stanton's statement and turned Sherman from diplomat to dupe, if not an outright traitor. In Washington, still full of conspiracy talk from the Lincoln assassination and attempts on other high federal officials the same night, some even spread the notion that Sherman planned to march north and make himself a military dictator, à la Julius Caesar.[20]

His letter to Ellen indicates that Sherman was, rather, concerned about getting his back pay and time off.[21] What was being said about him up North remained unknown to Sherman as he waited for the government's response. His engineers restored rail service and telegraph connections to Weldon, on the Virginia line. Sherman reviewed some of his troops, including the first black unit he had seen "as part of an organized army." Union cavalry remained in Durham's Station and Chapel Hill—where Union general Smith T. Atkins was about to create a scandal by courting University of North Carolina president David Swain's daughter, Ellie—and all in all the armies kept status quo.

Grant arrived on Monday, April 24. Sherman sent Johnston notice that their truce would expire in forty-eight hours and demanded Johnston's surrender, "on the same terms as were given to General Lee at Appomattox, April 9th instant, purely and simply."[22] Among them:

- Acts of war on the part of Johnston's command to cease;
- Troops to turn weapons over to the Union army;
- Every Confederate soldier to take a loyalty oath to the United States;
- Officers could keep their sidearms, personal horses and baggage;
- Former Confederates could go home and would be left alone by Federal forces as long as they were law-abiding.

Grant reviewed what Sherman wrote and gave his approval before it was sent. At the same time, Sherman issued orders for his own command to get ready for action in two days' time and wrote polite letters to Grant and to Stanton explaining his earlier conversations with Johnston and defending his decisions. To Grant, he further said: "I do believe we could and can

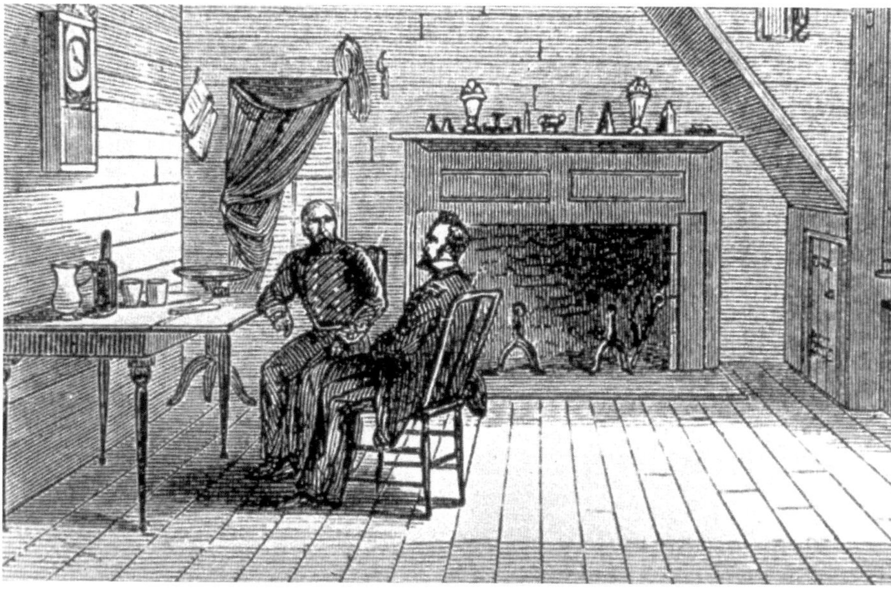

Generals Sherman and Johnston negotiate peace terms in the Bennitt farmhouse, April 1865. *Courtesy Bennett Place State Historic Site.*

use the present State governments lawfully, constitutionally, and as the very best possible means to produce the object desired, viz., entire and complete submission to the lawful authority of the United States." To Stanton: "I still believe the General Government of the United States has made a mistake; but that is none of my business."[23]

Receiving Sherman's notes, Johnston asked to meet again. Jefferson Davis had accepted the earlier terms, but when he saw the ultimatum of April 24 he ordered Johnston to have his infantry scatter and regroup later on at a place to be announced and to send what cavalry he had left to escort the Confederate president and governmental remnants out of Union reach. But when Johnston met Sherman for the third time at Bennitt's farm, he exceeded his authority again—and gave up the fight then and there even though some of his subordinates, notably cavalry commander Wade Hampton, were eager to resume the field.[24]

As far as Johnston was concerned, carrying on the war would be a pointless waste of lives. His army was hemorrhaging manpower throughout the lull in fighting, some commanders even giving their men leave to desert rather than suffer the embarrassment of surrendering. One command went from 1,600 men to 300 in ten days. The Rebels were hungry and barefoot, wearing rags and infested with lice.[25] Bromfield Ridley, one of Johnston's officers, recorded the mood in camp the night that surrender was announced: "All is confusion and unrest, and the stern realization that we are subdued, and ruined, is upon us. The proud spirited Southern people, all in a state of the veriest, the most sublimated sorrow...Confucius says 'our greatest glory is not in the never failing, but in rising every time we fall.'"[26]

That same night in Raleigh, there were fireworks and singing, but if Sherman was in any mood to celebrate it was likely tempered when he saw the *New York Times* accounts of what Stanton had released and the newspaper's commentary. Sherman hated the press, but this time his indignation was directed at the secretary of war, in a letter to U.S. Grant on April 28:

> *I do think that my Rank, if not past services, entitled me at least to the respect of Keeping secret what was Known to none but the Cabinet, until further inquiry could be made...To the courtesy of being consulted before publishing to the world a proposition rightfully submitted to higher authority for proper adjudication and then accompanied by other statements which invited the Press to be let loose on me.*

Sherman closed with something close to a warning, if not a premonition: "I envy not the task of reconstruction, and am delighted the Secretary [of War] has relieved me of it...[I] will with intense satisfaction leave to the Civil authorities the execution of the task of which they Seem to me so Jealous. But as an honest man and a soldier I invite them to follow my path, for they may see some things, and hear some things that may disturb their Philosophy."[27]

Written the same day, a letter to Ellen Sherman was more direct and ominous: "I perceive the Politicians are determined to drive the Confederates into Guerilla bands, a thing more to be feared than open organized war. They may fight it out—I wont. We could settle the war in three weeks by giving shape to the present disordered elements, but they may play out their game."[28]

NEW REGIME

So began Reconstruction. Sherman himself left North Carolina on Saturday, April 29. The same day, most of his army began the march home, leaving behind two corps and Major General John M. Schofield, whom Sherman had earlier appointed to oversee the Confederate paroles and reestablish order.

Born in New York, raised in Illinois and educated at West Point, Schofield distinguished himself at the Battle of Wilson's Creek, Missouri, in 1862—a Union defeat, but Schofield won a Medal of Honor for his part in the day—and as a manager who mediated tensions between abolitionists and less radical members of his command. In January 1865, he led the campaign that captured Fort Fisher, a massive Confederate fort protecting Wilmington, North Carolina, the last port open for blockade runners to supply the South from the outside world. From Wilmington, Schofield marched north to rendezvous with Sherman in March before the final advance on Raleigh.

One of the first to tell Schofield how to do his job was Salmon P. Chase, former U.S. secretary of the treasury whom Lincoln had appointed the U.S. Supreme Court's chief justice in 1864. Chase was a determined advocate of immediate suffrage for the former slaves and encouraged Schofield to embrace such a policy in North Carolina. Schofield, a centrist actually on the ground, objected on both legal and practical grounds in a May 10 letter to U.S. Grant:

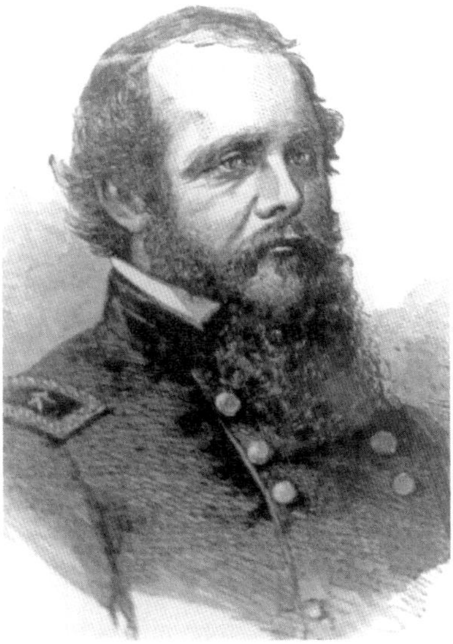

General John Schofield took command in North Carolina after Sherman and recommended caution on freedmen's vote. *Courtesy Bennett Place State Historic Site.*

> *The United States cannot make a negro, nor even a white man, an elector in any State. That is a power expressly reserved by the Constitution to the several States. We cannot alter or amend the constitution of North Carolina as it now exists without either first altering or else violating the Constitution of the United States...My second reason for objecting to the proposition is the absolute unfitness of the negroes, as a class, for any such responsibility. They can neither read nor write; they have no knowledge whatever of law or government...We certainly ought to teach them something before we give them an equal voice with ourselves in Government...A government so organized would in no sense be a popular government.*[29]

Two days later, in Washington, Andrew Johnson created the Bureau of Refugees, Freedmen and Abandoned Lands—later, simply "Freedmen's Bureau." Somebody else with the freedmen's situation on his mind was William Holden. Even before Johnston's surrender was final, Holden wrote in his newspaper:

> *One of the most difficult and perplexing questions to be settled is the relation which must subsist in the future in this state between the white and black populations. Everyone agrees that slavery will cease to exist, but the question now is, What must be the relative condition of the two races for the next few months? And, What must be the ultimate status of the colored race?*
>
> *The negro is not to blame for any of the sufferings entailed upon him by this war. It is not his fault that the children of Washington have been destroying each other in battle, nor can he reproach himself with the reflection that he has contributed either by word or deed to the privations and sufferings he is now enduring...He has strong claims on the sympathy of every right thinking person.*

> *Governor Brownlow, of Tennessee, whose judgment in all matters is entitled to respect, is in favor of providing for the colored race a separate and appropriate amount of territory, and settling them down permanently as a nation of freedmen,—and there is much force and propriety, it seems to us, in this suggestion, for the two races could not well live in harmony together as free races; but the question still presents itself, What must meanwhile be the condition of the colored race?*[30]

Lincoln's Emancipation Proclamation had freed all slaves in areas still rebellious as of January 1863, but the Thirteenth Amendment abolishing the practice had not been ratified, and the Fourteenth Amendment to guarantee former slaves' citizenship was more than two years away. Thus, Stanton's contention was that the Sherman-Johnston terms might have allowed for slavery's reestablishment and for divergent views on black voting.

Holden was a rather mercurial figure in North Carolina politics. Buying the *Standard* in 1843, he became a mouthpiece for and kingmaker in the state Democratic Party, even though he began his publishing career as an outspoken Whig. As tensions built between South and North, he remained a solid defender of states' rights—until secessions actually began, at which point he started recommending caution. Finding himself then on one side in a split party, he organized what he called a "Conservative" Party—not to be confused with the later Conservative Party of Reconstruction—in opposition to Jefferson Davis's administration in Richmond. In June 1863, Holden began calling for peace negotiations—before Vicksburg's fall and Lee's Gettysburg disaster turned battlefield momentum to the Union side for good.

As such, he riled up a great many North Carolinians and members of the Southern armed forces. In September 1863, a Georgia unit passing through Raleigh went to see Holden and set him straight. Not finding the editor at home, the soldiers marched to his newspaper office, broke down the door and ransacked the place, finally pouring printer's ink all over the wreckage. They were dissuaded from further action when Governor Zebulon Vance—to whom Holden had appealed for help, having heard he was in harm's way—appeared. Vance being a former soldier himself, the boys obeyed when he sent them back to camp. But a few nights later, a group of antiwar Raleigh citizens returned the favor by smashing up the pro-Confederate *State Journal* office.[31]

Passions remained warm, though with the prospect of Confederate defeat appearing more likely all the time and the tales and then experience of Sherman's march as reality check, war's end was generally welcomed,

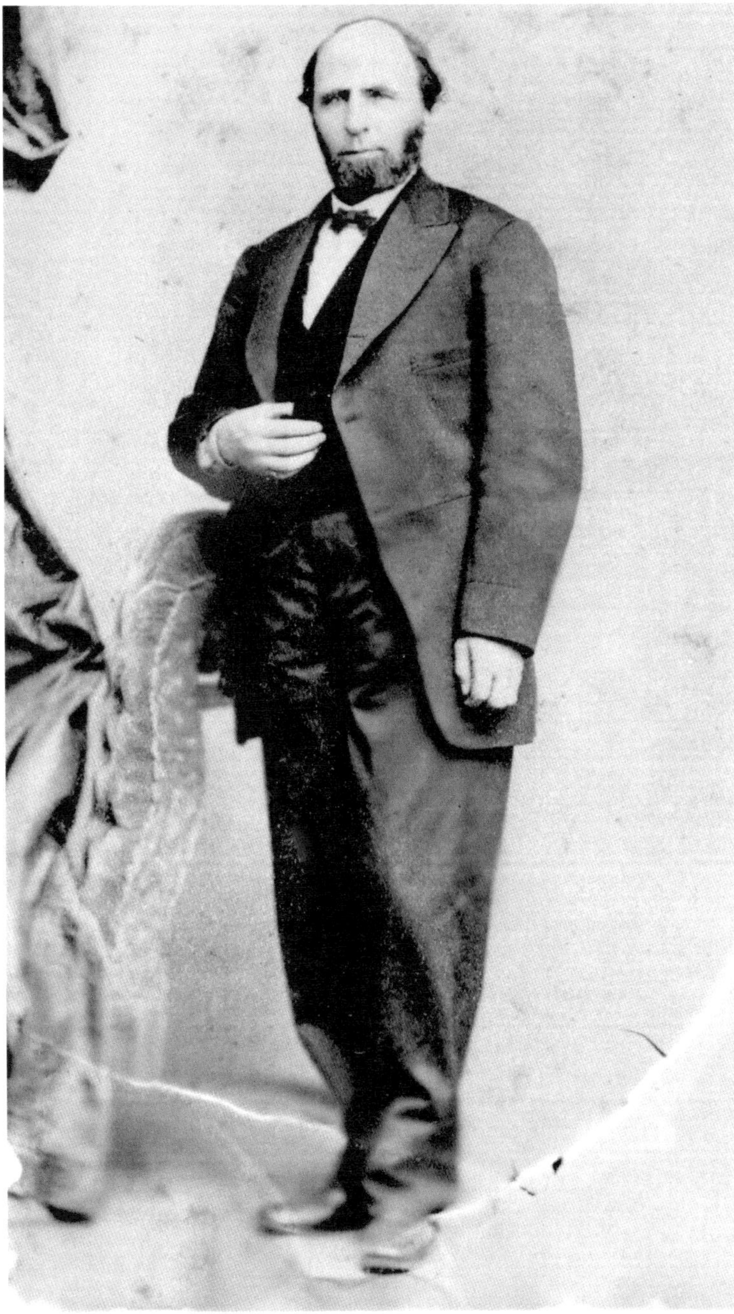

North Carolina *Standard* editor William Woods Holden in 1865. *Courtesy the North Carolina State Archives.*

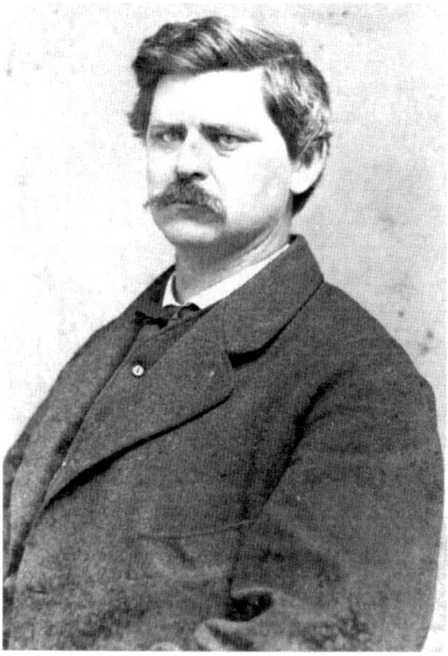

Zebulon Baird Vance, Confederate veteran and North Carolina governor at Civil War's end. *Courtesy the North Carolina State Archives.*

even if it did leave a somber and uncomfortable job ahead for North Carolina and the South in general. To a degree, reconstruction—not to be confused with Reconstruction—was quick to get underway. In Greensboro, Letitia Morehead Walker documented the arrival of occupation troops: "At sunset each evening the practicing of the various bands of music would again open the floodgates of [Southerners'] tears. But with the morning sun the avaricious desire for their 'greenbacks' seized the ladies of the town; chicken and fruit pies, beaten biscuits, ice cream, and cake poured through the camps."[32]

In Raleigh, Schofield lifted military restrictions on commerce in North Carolina, except for that in arms, ammunition, railroad and telegraph equipment and gray cloth. He reported that 37,011 officers and men of Johnston's army had received paroles, though Union forces at Greensboro had been unable to collect all the Confederates' arms and other public property, "and we were compelled to receive them wherever the troops chose to throw them down."[33]

In his May 10 letter to Grant, Schofield recommended that Washington appoint a military governor for the state who would decree that the pre-secession state constitution was in effect again—insofar as it was consistent with the United States Constitution—to appoint provisional state officers, such as justices of the peace and sheriffs, and to compile a registration list of voters who had sworn an amnesty oath.[34] Once registered, the voters should elect a state assembly to restore normal relations with the federal government, repeal the "pretended act of secession," outlaw slavery and take care of whatever other business was pressing—its actions to be submitted for popular referendum at the same time as election for a civilian governor and legislature.

> *The people are now ripe for action. They only ask to know what the Government desires for them to do, and how they are to do it. If, however,*

> *they should fail to do this, I would regard them as having violated their oaths, would dissolve the convention, and hold the State under military government until the people should come to their senses.*[35]

Holden, too, had advice to offer about government post-bellum. Even before Johnston's final surrender, the *Standard* was campaigning against reinstatement of the Vance administration, which had left town in advance of Sherman's arrival. Holden called their departure a de facto "abdication" and wrote that such "Destructives" were, politically, "doomed men for all time to come."[36]

In their place, he suggested that Andrew Johnson appoint a provisional governor to cooperate with the military "to restore order among the people, to enforce the laws, and to suppress that terrible guerilla warfare which is already afflicting the State, and which unless suppressed by the strong hand, will complete the ruin of every neighborhood." Like Schofield, Holden suggested a state convention to put the state back in proper line with the federal government, abolish slavery and arrange an election for state officials and delegates to Congress.[37]

Nothing if not attuned to political winds, Holden also promoted local meetings to organize a Union Party to aid and abet federal reconstruction once Washington decided what forms that would take. Circulating widely, the *Standard* inspired Unionist gatherings around the state, and their reports back to the paper gave the impression of a massing movement. Speaking at a rally, Holden ticked off the troubles facing North Carolina and sounded a call to look future- and Union-ward:

> *Prevention of secession was absolutely impossible in this State. I with others signed the ordinance of secession under the force of unavoidable circumstances. Union men, bowed down and stricken in spirit, silently acquiesced, while secessionists greeted the act with hats off and hurrahs, the firing of cannon and the ringing of bells.*
>
> *Now, fellow citizens, what remains but to address ourselves to our duties as loyal citizens and to improve and build up our native State?...To our brethren of the North and East and West we say, come over and help us. Bring your capital, your muscle, your intelligence, your industry, your ingenuity, and settle among us. The way is now open, and with us and our children you can purchase and build, and plant and reap, and repose and labor, and live and die, leaving your possessions an assured inheritance, for I tell you that the stars in that banner will never go out, and the sun of*

American liberty will never go down. Our banner staff is at last so firmly planted that no convulsion which did not split the earth could upheave it from its place.[38]

He had also assured his readers that, with the new administration on the Potomac, they were in good hands. Of Johnson, he wrote:

A native of this City, and…eminently a self-made man. We know him well. He is a man of first-rate ability, possessed of an iron will, and enthusiastically devoted, as his whole public life shows, to the rights and interests of the people. We believe he will make a safe and able President. He will have the warm sympathies of the people of his native state, and their earnest prayers that his administration may promote the happiness of the whole American people.[39]

Johnson was, indeed, a self-made man. His parents, Jacob and Mary, worked at Casio's Inn, a Raleigh watering hole popular with the legislative set. Jacob was also the capitol building's janitor. Andrew, born in 1808, never went to school but taught himself to read while serving as a tailor's apprentice. After his master sold his business, Johnson moved to Tennessee, and by the time he was twenty-one he had already won election as a Greeneville alderman.

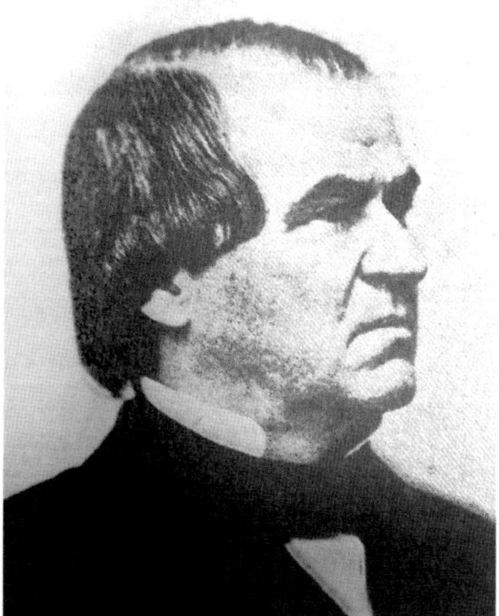

Andrew Johnson, a native of Raleigh, provided a mild Reconstruction plan that Congress overturned. *Courtesy Library of Congress.*

Johnson may or may not have seen anything Holden wrote about him or about reconstruction, but on May 9 Johnson telegraphed the Raleigh editor, "Can you come to Washington immediately? I wish to confer with you in reference to North Carolina affairs."[40]

North Carolina affairs were not in good shape. The state was $40 million in debt. Civil authority was still broken, and wherever Union troops did not enforce a semblance of order, anarchy was in charge. Walking home to Tennessee, Bromfield Ridley and his companions had trouble with "stragglers" who tried to take their mules and found forage hard to come by—though civilians who had food to trade were glad to swap for spun thread.[41]

Banks were busted, bridges were burned, warehouses were looted, farms were untended. At the thirty-thousand-acre Cameron plantations in Orange County, liberated slaves feasted on the food stocks that had been put away for safekeeping, emptied the smokehouses and slaughtered the livestock; owner Paul Cameron wrote that "all are going to the devil or dogs as fast as they can."[42] Some occupation forces added to the miseries left by renegade Confederates. In Alamance County, an infantry detachment camping at a formerly prosperous farm burned its fences and orchards, shot sheep and hogs on the spot, drove wagons across ripening fields and made off with all the horses and cattle.[43] At the university in Chapel Hill, only ten or twelve students remained, and there were but four graduates at a somber commencement where the only visitors were Union soldiers assigned to maintain order. Even the university president, former governor David Swain, was away—in Washington with several other of North Carolina's leading men to have a talk of their own with the president.[44]

Johnson and his cabinet had taken up his native state's situation on May 8. Stanton suggested a military government, with a provisional civil authority to be constituted sometime down the line. Johnson dodged talking about black voting rights for the moment and said that further studies were called for. The next day, he wired Holden to come see him and bring along any friends he thought would be of use.

They reached Washington on May 18 and right away went into conference with Johnson. At the same time, Swain and several other friends of the former Vance administration—but who had been Union sympathizers before the war began—had come to the capital on their own to try and check Holden's influence. They told the president that he ought to reconvene the pre-surrender legislature and let it get reconstruction underway, rather than creating the provisional government as Schofield and Holden favored. Their idea went nowhere; Johnson had already made up his mind to go provisional, and anyway, it was too much like the Sherman-Johnston proposal that Stanton, and Johnson, had already rejected.[45]

Swain had one more move to try. The North Carolina groups met with Johnson together on May 25. The president showed them a proclamation he had drafted to set the reconstruction agenda in their state, leaving a blank space for the governor's name. Then he left the room. Swain walked out, too, followed by Holden—who had unsuccessfully run for governor the year before and might not have wanted to give the impression that he was after the office again. He caught up with Swain, and they walked together for a ways before the former governor advised Holden not to accept the job if it were offered. Holden was a divisive figure, as the presence in Washington of the two delegations demonstrated, and Swain thought that the state would be better off with someone else in charge. Holden misinterpreted what the diplomatic Swain said, though, and assumed that he was concerned for the university and that Holden, not a college man himself, might not be an ardent supporter of the school. Holden replied that he might or might not get appointed governor, but either way, "I am your friend, and the friend of Chapel Hill."[46]

That established, the two men returned to the White House, where Holden's friends had written in his name. The following day, Johnson made the appointment official and issued a proclamation for reconstruction in North Carolina that was a template for his program throughout the former Confederacy. He directed Holden, as provisional governor, to convene an assembly "chosen by that portion of the people of said State who are loyal to the United States, and no others," to do what was necessary "to restore said State to its constitutional relations to the Federal Government" and provide for the state "a republican form of government."

Moreover, Johnson decreed that in subsequent elections no one would be eligible to vote, or hold state office, without taking an amnesty oath and unless they were qualified under the state laws in effect before secession. The proclamation ordered military authorities to assist the provisional government and provide for reestablishing postal service, a federal court and tax collection in the state.[47] Defining eligibility in terms of 1861 state law bypassed the touchy black voting question—no doubt disappointing Washington radicals, such as Chief Justice Chase, who were pressing Johnson to make suffrage a cornerstone for reconstructing and redefining the South.[48]

Holden's accession was not met with universal enthusiasm back home. In her diary, Catherine Ann Edmondston of Halifax County gentility called the new governor "a base born bastard with neither the breeding or the instincts of a gentleman." An old Whig named A.M. McPheeters, perhaps blessed with a long memory, declared, "I regard Holden now, as I have done for years past, as a bad man, entirely devoid of principle." To his opponents, the secessionist-turned-Union man appeared no more than a power-hungry opportunist; some even expected him to launch a "reign of terror and persecution" against anyone who had opposed him in the past.[49]

The new governor did attempt some fence-mending, appointing Vance's secretary of state, Charles Thomas, and treasury secretary, Jonathan Worth, to their old jobs. Worth was an old Unionist who had a reputation for scrupulous honesty. In the *Standard*, Holden praised his new appointment: "It will give the citizens of the entire State great satisfaction to know that Mr. Worth is to discharge its duty. His judgment, energy, and integrity mark him as the man who will perform them for the best interest of the State." Holden had already turned the newspaper over to his son Jo and political ally Joseph S. Cannon; he had plenty else to occupy his time.

> *I was closely and constantly engaged, and found I had undertaken a very heavy task indeed. I had able assistants who helped me very much, but I had to conceive, and plan, and do everything in the way of reconstructing the State. For the first months I had not less than seventy-five visitors every day, which engaged my attention for hours, for the most part of the time, in fact. I had to provide books with the Amnesty oaths for all the counties, to appoint persons in various counties to administer those oaths, to obtain horses and mules for applicants by applying to the military, and settle disputes between men in regard to property of various kinds, to correspond on matters of business which required attention, and in all respects to work, work, work.*[50]

Holden's detractors criticized him for being slow to call the prescribed state convention, but the governor really had his hands full. He was the first provisional governor actually in office, and he had no guidelines or models for what he was supposed to do, other than the wartime state governments set up as the Union won control of previously Confederate territory.[51] He had eighty-seven county and myriad town governments to organize, local disputes to settle and thousands of officials to appoint and, in some cases, remove from office and replace. Some regions remained in a state of anarchy. Schofield had delegated some troops to act as local police and appointed a few magistrates, bringing a degree of law and order in some places, but the jurisdictional line between state and federal courts remained to be defined. In the western mountains, citizens who had remained on the Union side took the opportunity to get even with Rebel sympathizers who had tormented them during the war. And there were those residents to deal with who had fallen outside the scope of the president's general amnesty.[52]

> *I received every day a large number of applications for pardon which I read carefully. I was the medium through which these applications went to the President, and my duty was to mark them Granted, Postponed, or Rejected. Not that I did that, but they were thus marked for the President. It was with him to grant, postpone, or reject them. During my time of seven months about twelve hundred pardons (1200) as well as I recollect, were thus obtained from the President. I asked him during all this time to reject but four; some were postponed, and many granted.*[53]

Pardon remained a presidential prerogative. Holden could only recommend Johnson's approval of a pardon application, which he did in 1,451 out of 1,555 cases. What happened to applications after they left his desk, though, was subject to Washington bureaucracy and the applicant's direct appeal of a Holden rejection to the White House. Johnson was sometimes slow in getting around to signing pardons, for he was just as swamped with demands and pressures as his provisional governors, and even the presence of Holden's appointed lobbyist, Robert J. Powell, in the capital could not expedite matters.

In retrospect, Holden's handling of the provisional assignment has received generally high marks. Even the historian Joseph Gregoire de Roulhac Hamilton, a harsh critic of Holden in the early twentieth century, wrote:

> *Leaving out all question of motive in certain individual cases, his work was well done. He was less proscriptive than might have been expected…in view of the events of the preceding five years, and he showed consideration for the feelings of his opponents by securing* [Confederate governor Zebulon] *Vance's release on parole on account of the illness of his wife, and by various other acts to which his kindly nature impelled him.*[54]

Holden actually caught criticism from some of his fellow Unionists for filling some offices with men whom he considered capable despite their support for Vance in 1864 and/or roles as prominent secessionists in 1861. They thought that such appointments would lead to a state constitutional convention that undid much of what the war had won. When complaints began reaching ears in Washington, along with similar reports from other Southern states, Johnson issued a statement that dismissed them as attempts to embarrass his government.[55]

Holden took the statement as a personal slight on the job he was doing, writing the president:

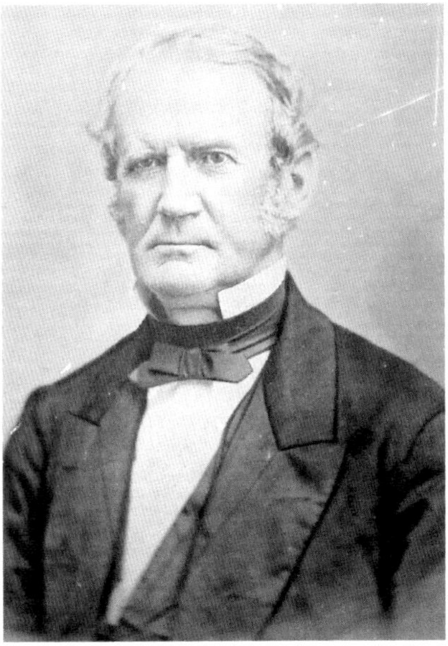

William Alexander Graham, Holden's childhood benefactor and adult antagonist. *Courtesy Library of Congress.*

> *There are no grounds for apprehending that North Carolina will not present an acceptable constitution. The great body of her people are loyal and submissive... There are malcontents, radicals, and not good men who are engaged in misrepresenting facts, and fermenting strife for certain purposes; but none of these things move me in the performance of duty.*[56]

Holden left himself open to charges of playing politics with pardons. When the former governor and United States senator William A. Graham appealed his application pardon to Washington, Holden intervened and blocked the old Whig for months. Thomas Bragg, another former governor and senator, although a Democrat, got a similar treatment. Former Whig lawyer Josiah Turner Jr., a Holden ally in opposition to the Jeff Davis administration, became a raging Holden foe when the governor refused to tell him that he had recommended Turner's pardon be denied.[57] The refusal would drive Turner and stalk Holden for the rest of their lives.

ISSUES BLACK AND WHITE

While Holden was occupied creating a government in Raleigh, others were doing their parts to shape the South's, and North Carolina's, new identity.

Chief Justice Salmon P. Chase was not only a longtime abolitionist but also a strong advocate for black suffrage. Early in 1865, he had said that leaving blacks disenfranchised would be "a crime and a folly," leaving "colored loyalists" in the control of former Rebels, and with the war over he lobbied Andrew Johnson to make black voting part of his reconstruction plan right away.

With Johnson hesitant to push the just-subdued South and much of the North that far, Chase set off to examine the freedmen's condition himself. His party stopped in North Carolina, South Carolina and Florida, with Chase writing back to the president on what he saw and what Johnson ought to do about it. Confirmed in his beliefs after interviewing military officials, local politicians, former slaves and even some former slave owners, he advised a strong presidential push for universal manhood suffrage, whatever white citizens thought about it. Many whites disliked the idea, but Chase claimed that enough would go along in the interest of peace to overcome the opposition. As for blacks themselves, he wrote Johnson, "They attach very great importance to the right of voting," politically adding, "They form a power which no wise Statesman will disregard."[58]

As if to underline that point, Chase reported that, everywhere he went, the freedmen were organizing Union Leagues. The first Union

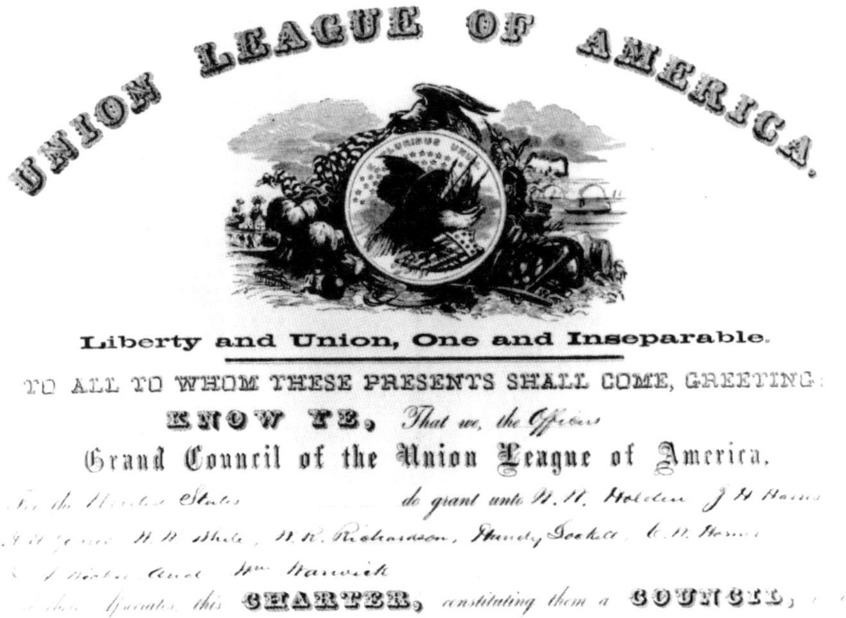

UNION LEAGUE OF AMERICA.

Liberty and Union, One and Inseparable.

TO ALL TO WHOM THESE PRESENTS SHALL COME, GREETING:

KNOW YE, That we, the Officers

Grand Council of the Union League of America,

CHARTER, constituting them a COUNCIL,

North Carolina Union League Charter, naming W.W. Holden as one of its officers. *Courtesy the North Carolina State Archives.*

League club had been founded in Philadelphia in 1862, growing out of a movement to rebuild support for the Union cause that was flagging in the North as Confederates won one battle after another. The movement spread during the war, becoming in essence an auxiliary of the Republican Party's radical wing. Within the Confederacy, its counterpart was the Heroes of America, commonly known as "Red Strings" for the cords they wore to identify one another. A secret society supplying intelligence to the North and aid to unwilling conscripts and escaped Yankee prisoners, the Red Strings were particularly strong in North Carolina, and Holden's *North Carolina Standard* was reputed to be its mouthpiece in the central part of the state[59]—a reputation Holden's opponents used to good effect in the gubernatorial campaign of 1864, despite the editor's vehement denials.[60] After the war, it continued to operate, like the Union League helping to organize blacks as a political force and gaining the enmity of white supremacists.

Even Chase was cautionary about blacks' voting prospects. During his Southern tour, a North Carolina editor told him that the state's whites would oppose black suffrage and "should the general government attempt to force it upon them, they would feel aggrieved and mortified."[61] Addressing a freedmen's gathering in Charleston, he told his audience that a vote in peace was the equivalent of a bayonet in war but added that the right to vote, if gained soon, must not be abused. If it was not gained right away, he told the freedmen, they would have to be patient, meanwhile conducting themselves in a manner to inspire confidence that they were ready to take on citizenship's authority.[62]

In Raleigh, Holden had similar counsel. In his first formal address to the state as provisional governor, he had special words for the freedmen:

> *Your race has been depressed by your condition of slavery, and by the legislation of your former masters for two hundred years. It is not to be expected that you can comprehend and appreciate as they should be comprehended by a self-governing people, the wise provisions and limitations of the Constitution and the laws; or that you can now have that knowledge of public affairs which is necessary to qualify you to discharge all the duties of citizens. No people has ever yet bounded at once into the full enjoyment of the right of self-government...*
>
> *Freedom does not mean that one may do as he pleases, but that everyone may, by industry, frugality, and temperance, improve his conditions and enjoy the fruits of his own labors...I will set my pace against those of you who are idle and dissipated, and prompt punishment will be inflicted for any breach of the peace or violation of the law.*[63]

There's hardly room to doubt that Holden chose some of his words to comfort his white public as well as, if not more than, to inspire his black public, who were not sure themselves just what "freedom" meant for them. Clearly, it meant that they were no longer obligated by law to do as white masters dictated; but neither were their former masters bound to them by economic self-interest, if not common humanity. Some former slaves, confronted with decisions to make on their own as well as opportunity to make them, stayed put; some hit the road looking for opportunity, friends or family or simply enjoying the liberty to go where they liked. Where slaves and free blacks had attended the same churches as their owners or white neighbors before emancipation, now they deserted those denominations and congregations in favor of founding their own. Freed slaves organized meetings, acquired weapons and otherwise flaunted their independence in such ways as refusing to give way to whites in the street.[64]

Naturally enough, such behaviors gave whites pause and frequently motivated whites to let the freedmen know they weren't as free as they might have thought. Racist ideology, the notion of blacks' inherent mental and moral inferiority to whites, was conventional wisdom in both North and South and had been drummed ever deeper into the Southern psyche by decades of political rhetoric in defense of slavery. Moreover, whites had learned to be afraid of organized and armed blacks after bloody slave insurrections in South Carolina and Virginia. That fear could only have strengthened during the war; in December 1864, rumors of a slave rising planned for Christmas Eve had the white population of Richmond County, on the South Carolina line, in a near panic that led to three slaves being lynched and many more thrown into jail.

Pauli Murray, a twentieth-century African American lawyer and priest whose grandfather came to the postwar South to teach in a freedmen's school near Hillsborough, North Carolina, wrote of that time in a family memoir:

> *New bridges of communication must be built between whites and blacks, too big a job to be done with hate, yet the war had left little among the defeated Rebels but piled-up hate. White men were determined that black men give them the same unquestioned obedience they had exacted before the war; black men were equally determined to be "treated just like white men." Until one of these urges gave way, undeclared war would continue.*[65]

Some prominent North Carolinians were prepared to accept black voting—though some, such as university president David Swain, qualified their support by limiting the black vote to contests for the state House of Commons or otherwise granting only a partial franchise. Some were willing to go all the way as a tactic to head off intervention in state affairs by a national government in which Republican radicals might gain control.

Freedmen didn't wait on white opinion. John P. Sampson, a Wilmington native who had escaped to Ohio and edited a newspaper for blacks there, came back to North Carolina in the summer of 1865 to help a suffrage campaign and organize a statewide freedmen's convention in Raleigh. Representatives from forty-two counties appeared. Freedom was new to most of the 117 delegates and most were illiterate, but they established themselves and the race as a force in state politics. In a petition for the constitutional convention, the assembly called for North Carolina to grant them full citizenship along with access to schools, to rescind discriminatory laws, protect families and orphans, encourage black industry and provide food and shelter until blacks could support themselves.[66]

The latter was asking a lot from a state devastated, directly or indirectly, by the war. Murray, relying perhaps on her imagination as well as family stories, describes the country her grandfather came to as in a "desolation of peace," a realm of abandoned fields, burned farms, wrecked railroads and people "more ravished than the land." Their animals gone or dead, humans hitched themselves to plows if they had the will and energy to do more than move "as if under some strange hypnotic power...without thinking or feeling."

Many North Carolina residents survived only because occupation soldiers fed them. In Caswell County, before the war one of North Carolina's most bountiful agricultural producers, the diarist John F. Flintoff wrote in August:

> *The people have had scarcely bread to supply them till harvest fall—they will live on what there is—very little meat anywhere to be had...I am feeble as to health and only weigh 136 lost 12 lbs in 4 months tho I am still at work—My negroes all stay with me while the most of others are running about from home to home believing they are free—many of them are killed and dieing for want of money and protection—poor creatures—I have to ride often after them and arrest them for trial, for their fighting, stealing and other meanness they are very troublesome to white people.*[67]

Into this volatile situation strode another catalyst from outside: Albion W. Tourgee, abolitionist of Ohio. Tourgee was a twenty-eight-year-old Union veteran, a farm boy whose parents gave him a strict Methodist upbringing but also gave him a taste for ideas and argument that led to a rebel streak and a degree of self-righteousness acknowledged even by later admirers. "He hated with perfect hatred anything that savored of dandyism or of a dilettante attitude toward life and attacked it with unrelenting acerbity," wrote the biographer Roy F. Dibble in 1921.[68] He also had a tendency to let wishful imagination color his own accounts of his life.[69]

Adopting an intense opposition to slavery from his wife-to-be, Emma Kilbourne—a descendant of New England Tories—Tourgee was an active Lincoln supporter as a campus politico at the University of Rochester and joined the Union army in time to get a severe spinal injury at the Battle of First Manassas (aka Bull Run) in June 1865. He recovered, returned to active duty and spent time in three Southern prisoner of war

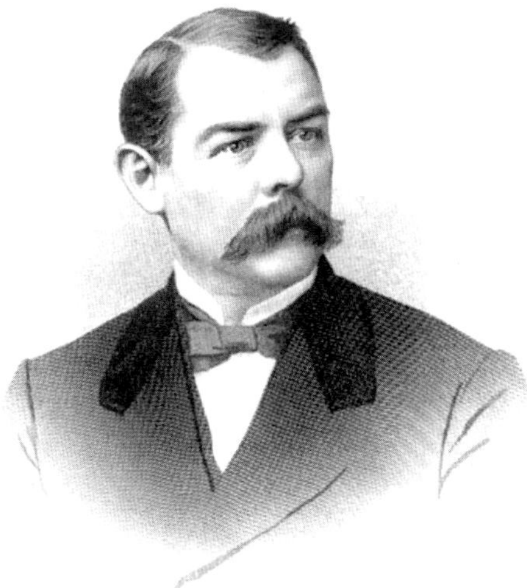

Albion Winegar Tourgee planned to remake the South in the Northern image. He met resistance. *Courtesy Caswell County Historical Association.*

camps, and his sympathies for African Americans were only strengthened by the experience. Before the Emancipation Proclamation of 1863, Tourgee had formed the opinion that he was fighting not merely to maintain the Union but also, perhaps more important to him, for racial equality.[70] And when he went south in 1865, it was not with the idea of merely joining the reconstruction but of starting the South's social order all over again to suit his own ideals. In Southern terms he was, to put it politely, a carpetbagger.

Of course, Tourgee was far from unusual and far from the first Yankee to head South with missionary intent and zeal. Almost as soon as Northern forces won back Rebel real estate, teachers from abolitionist hotbeds such as Massachusetts were on their way to staff the new freedmen's schools and enlighten the former slaves with not just reading and writing but also a Puritan work ethic and the spirit of capitalism.

Restless after his army discharge, Tourgee cast about for something to do with himself. He completed the law studies he had started while recuperating from his war injury, was admitted to the Ohio bar and then settled for a while into teaching school in Pennsylvania and occasionally writing for newspapers. Then he realized that the beaten South was a land of opportunity with better weather. North Carolina seemed a likely spot, given its relatively large Unionist population, so the hopeful reformer got in touch with the Unionist governor, William Holden.

Holden had already invited the rest of the country to bring its muscle and ingenuity down south, and responding to Tourgee's letter in June 1865, he encouraged him to join the rest. Land was cheap, greenbacks could buy a lot—but he did advise that the state needed the North's skilled labor because too many native blacks were "unskilled and uncertain." After meeting Holden in person and gaining introductions to some influential people, Tourgee decided to settle in north-centrally located Guilford County, where a large, long-established Quaker population was already setting up freedmen's schools of its own. Welcomed there, Tourgee and two college friends leased a nursery farm near Greensboro and formed a corporation to invest in other Southern ventures and practice law, while hiring black farmhands to tend their fruit trees and plant stock—in the process, acquiring the habits and learning the value of Northern-style free labor.

North Carolina was a beaten Southern state, but it was not as uniformly hostile to Tourgee and at least some of his ideas as might be supposed. The state had a history of prizing individual liberty—refusing to ratify the U.S. Constitution until the Bill of Rights was added—and of internal dissention. In 1781, back-country "Regulators" staged an armed insurrection over what they considered abuses by the provincial government; during the Revolutionary War, Patriots and Tories carried on guerilla warfare motivated as much by opportunism and personal grudge as by political inclination; in the antebellum decades, the state enjoyed a lively political scene with Democrats and Whigs contesting for power; and while generally upholding slavery (except for the large Quaker population in the central, or Piedmont, section), the state was passionately divided over secession—becoming the last to leave the Union, in May 1865.

During the War Between the States, the value put on personal liberty led many North Carolinians—prominently, William Holden—to oppose the Richmond government for its infringements on civil rights such as the writ of habeas corpus. Some of the state's prominent politicians retained their Unionist sympathies, and others who had gone with the Confederacy were ready to change their minds as the war went more and more against the South. So, by 1865, there was considerable sentiment to put the Confederacy behind and adjust to new reality. At least, to a point.

Local Unionists turned out to be some of Tourgee's first clients in Greensboro, the Guilford County seat. Ironically enough, they hired him to handle their claims for property damage inflicted by Sherman's Union soldiers. The legal practice led Tourgee to make close and harmonious contacts among his new neighbors—and, before too long, with a North Carolinian named John Walter Stephens, commonly known by the nickname "Chicken."[71]

While A.W. Tourgee & Co. was getting itself established, the governor was arranging the convention required by Johnson's May 29 decree to restore North Carolina "to its constitutional relations to the Federal Government, and to present such a republican form of State government as will entitle the State to the guarantee of the United States therefore, and its people to protection by the United States against invasion, insurrection, and domestic violence." On August 8, Holden made a proclamation for those citizens who had been pardoned to elect delegates and sent messengers across the state—mail and telegraph service still not fully operational—to spread the word.

Delegate selection was a calm process. As the future judge Robert Watson Winston recalled, at that time "those secessionists who had brought on the war were held in aversion,"[72] and with Unionists old and new alert for any power plays by the discredited old guard, they stayed out of the process. Of the 120 delegates, 46 had been Union sympathizers in early 1861, and all would go on to join the Republican Party.[73] Holden was pleased with the results, even asking Andrew Johnson to expedite pardons for 11 men elected despite the pardoned-only provision in Johnson's decree.

Holden arranged for the Capitol building's furniture, which had been removed during Sherman's occupation—probably to protect it from the vandalism that made a wreck of some other state offices—to be returned and put in place, and the delegates met on October 2. Though Johnson's decree did not expressly require it, everyone knew that the first order of business had to be retracting the May 21, 1861 act of secession and the outlawing of slavery, and the convention obliged within the week—though its resolutions would have to pass a public referendum. During that week, Holden presented the petition for equality from the freedmen's convention, which was then wrapping up. Holden said nothing about the petition one way or another, and it was quickly referred to a committee, which duly concluded that it was a matter best left for a future legislature to deal with.

Providing for that future legislature, the convention ruled that it should come to order in late November, its membership to be chosen along with a governor and other state officials by a special election earlier that month. To keep the state going, the convention levied more than a dozen new taxes. That left the delegates with one more matter to consider—what to do about the massive debt North Carolina had incurred while part of the wartime Confederacy. The prevailing sentiment, and the president's wish, was to simply repudiate it—the state was hard up enough without that on its books, too. But repudiation would ruin most of the state's banks, wipe out personal investments and eliminate the endowments for public schools and the university. A committee recommended putting that decision off, as well, but no sooner had it reported than, at Holden's behest, a motion to repudiate came to the floor. After several days' debate, the motion appeared likely to fail in favor of postponement. At that point, Holden appeared with a telegram—which he had requested—from Johnson stating that "every dollar of the debt created to aid the rebellion" had to be "repudiated finally and forever" or North Carolina and any other state not so obliging would be barred from reentering the Union.[74]

Repudiation passed, the convention adjourned until the following May and, election day having been set for November 9, the politicking began. Already, fifty-three of Holden's friends among the convention delegates had formally requested that he stand for governor, "being desirous that restoration should be completed by one under whose guidance it has been so auspiciously begun,"[75] and knowing that their man had craved election for years. As expected, Holden thanked the petitioners and accepted the call:

> *I have been content to do my duty to the best of my ability under the instructions of the President, and to leave my conduct to be judged by an intelligent and indulgent people. I do not fear that judgment…My paramount concern has been, so to do that part of the work assigned to me as to secure the restoration of the State to the Union at the earliest practicable period. To what extent I have succeeded in this respect it is for the people to say. I can only declare, as I most solemnly do, that I have labored with an eye single to the good and the glory of North Carolina; and that, whatever may be the decision of the people on the 9th of November, I shall always possess the consciousness that I am a faithful and devoted son of our dear old State, and that I have labored with zeal, and with what success my poor faculties could command, to improve the condition of her people, and to restore her to her appropriate and natural position in the Union.*

Whatever Holden thought about his job performance and motivation, there were more than a few people of North Carolina who thought very little of him—even among the convention delegates with whom he had been well pleased. Opposition coalesced around the provisional state treasurer, Jonathan Worth, a former Whig and a member of the peace movement during the war but also the man Holden himself had praised in the *Standard* for his judgment and integrity. During the campaign, Holden's side had claimed that its man's close relations with Andrew Johnson would ease North Carolina's way back into the Union, while Worth backers pointed out Holden's history of changing his mind and loyalties. Holden appealed to the president for his endorsement, claiming that "the money power" was against him for his role in debt repudiation and that if he lost, "a powerful party will at once exist against your administration."[76]

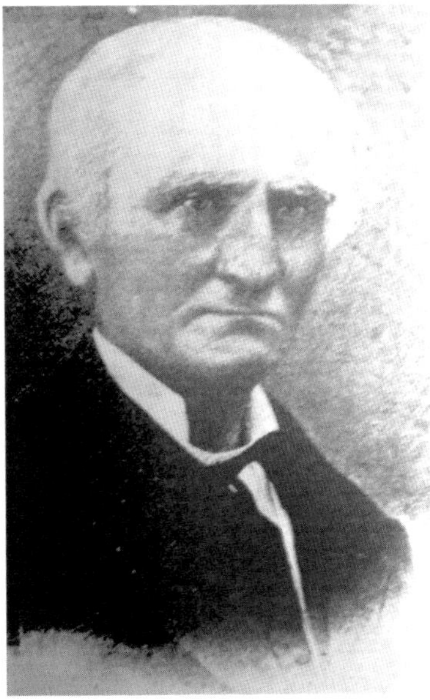

Jonathan Worth was Holden's choice for state treasurer, but he gave Worth the governor's seat with great reluctance. *From Hamilton's* History of North Carolina.

Johnson stayed out of North Carolina's politics, and Worth, his campaign managed by the infuriated Josiah Turner, won the election with more than 55 percent of the vote. Worth carried fifty-three counties; Holden only thirty-five. The lame-duck provisional governor took to his sickbed, though he had enough fight left to wire Johnson that the victors were Rebels at heart and "the copperhead now shows his fangs"—making reference to the North's Southern sympathizers during the war. Johnson responded to his ally's plaints with directions to maintain the provisional government until the state legislature ratified the Thirteenth Amendment, making slavery unconstitutional and with a telegram of praise for "the noble and efficient manner" by which he had managed the state. Johnson warned the citizens: "The results of the recent elections in North Carolina have greatly damaged the prospects of the State in the restoration of its governmental relations. Should the action and spirit of the legislature be in the same direction, it will greatly increase the mischief already done and might be fatal."[77]

Johnson's message had some effect: once met, the state General Assembly ratified the Thirteenth Amendment in short order. But Holden was hoping that his man in Washington would stall, or even deny, Worth's assumption of his seat. That didn't happen, but other powers in the capital did reject others duly elected.

Seven U.S. representatives were elected in November, but senators were to be named by the legislature. Holden was offered one of the two seats, but he turned it down. The legislators then voted John Pool, a plantation owner from the eastern part of the state who had run for governor as a Democrat and lost in 1860; and William A. Graham, whom Holden had alienated over the appealed pardon. Graham right away set off for Washington with the legislature's petition for his pardon in hand. Johnson's signature was necessary for Graham—who had been a Confederate congressman—to take his seat. Holden interceded to block the pardon again, advising the president that no Northern representative would accept an old Rebel in the hallowed halls of the United States Capitol. Johnson, wishing to hurry along his reconstruction program, signed the pardon, but Holden had been right. With Congress back in session as of early December, and the Radical Republicans ascendant, both of North Carolina's chosen senators were barred from taking their seats.

A showdown was shaping up over what version of Reconstruction the South would get: Johnson's or Congress's. The president, making a gesture of his own, began removing his provisional governments and turning the former Confederate states back to their own officials. Holden got the word to hand over his office to Worth by way of Secretary of State William Seward. Holden respond with his "copperhead" letter. Then, saying, "My chief wish is to be of benefit to my afflicted State," he handed over his office keys on December 28 and retired to his newspaper trade. For the time being.[78]

THE MAN WHO WOULD BE GOVERNOR

I was poor and unknown and very ambitious.
—*William Woods Holden,* Memoirs[79]

So who was this man Holden, this polarizing politician? Opportunist or visionary, villain or statesman? The *Dictionary of North Carolina Biography* describes him as a "printer, editor, politician, governor, and the most controversial state figure during Reconstruction."[80] There is no question that Holden was an adroit politician with a keen sense of the winds' directions and a well-honed sense of self-preservation. Nor is there any question that he recognized opportunity when it appeared and knew how to take advantage. But was he driven by sheer ambition, by a guiding sense of right and wrong, by state patriotism, by a chip on his shoulder? Was he a champion of the downtrodden or just a bearer of grudges out to bring the powerful low?

Probably some of all of these and maybe more. Posterity will never know, and honest self-examination not being particularly fashionable among Victorian Americans on the make, it's unlikely that Holden himself could have sorted out his motivations, or that it would have occurred to him to do so.

He was born on November 24, 1818, out of wedlock to Thomas W. Holden and Priscilla Woods. His status as a literal bastard apparently had little or nothing to do with the way the boy "Billy" was regarded in and around his hometown of Hillsborough, or by his parents. In later life, he would make reference to his own "unpretending origins" and his "inheritance of ignorance and poverty," but the circumstances of his birth did not bar him from the top ranks of North Carolina politics and society, and his childhood does not appear to have been particularly unusual for small-town early America.

Billy's grandfather, an English immigrant to the colonies, was a farmer in Orange County when it was still part of the Carolina backcountry—a region distant from the gentrified Tidewater in geography and culture. North Carolina does not offer good harbors like Virginia's Norfolk and South Carolina's Charleston. Most of the coast is blocked by barrier islands separated from one another by dangerous inlets and from the mainland by wide sounds too shallow to accommodate oceangoing ships of any size. The harbors that North Carolina did have were not particularly inviting: Beaufort, small and difficult to access from the interior; and Wilmington, guarded by treacherous currents and shoals that encouraged merchantmen to go elsewhere for berths. Consequently, commerce and capital tended to flow out of state, and English settlement was slow to migrate west from the few early coastal-plain enclaves.

Foreign populations did find their way to the interior, but by roundabout ways. At least as early as the 1660s, white Virginia traders were making contact with Indians to the west and south, and settlers discontented with the developing gentry establishment, runaway slaves and indentured servants and Europeans simply out for elbow room and adventure drifted inland into the Carolina wilds, where they mixed and mingled with one another and the natives, happily out of reach of His Majesty's government and church. Virginia royal governor Alexander Spotswood alerted the Lords Commanders of Trade in 1714 that to North Carolina "great numbers of loose and disorderly people daily flock"[81] The gentleman William Byrd, one of the surveyors marking the boundary between Virginia and North Carolina in 1728, commented on the colony to the south: "It approaches nearer to the Description of Lubberland than any other, by the great felicity of the Climate, the easiness of raising Provisions and the Slothfulness of the People…Tis a thorough Aversion to Labor that makes people file off to N. Carolina."[82] In response, North Carolinians have dubbed their state a "Vale of Humility Between Two Mountains of Conceit."

Nevertheless, a measure of British civilization had established itself in the backcountry by the 1740s in the form of formal titles to land and residents of record. Conditions remained somewhat wild, as attested by a traveler named J.F.D. Smyth's encounter with "insect[s], reptiles, and serpents of the most poisonous, deadly, and fatal nature, swarming in the woods, and on the ground, and the wild beasts howling hideously around me"; and the legislature's act for dispatching animals "injurious and prejudicial," such as wolves, panthers and bears, to citizens in the middle part of the state as late as 1785.[83] But clerics, sheriffs and lawyers were making their presence felt, along with increasing numbers of taxable subjects, such that Orange County was drawn upon the royal maps in 1752, covering the area later subdivided into Alamance, Caswell, Chatham, Durham, eastern Guilford, Person and a much-diminished Orange Counties. The new county was sanctified with a St. Matthew's Parish of the Church of England and brought to order with a tax of one shilling on every white male resident of any substance—according to a sheriff's count, there were 1,113 "tythables" available. Two years after the county's creation, surveyors laid out a town to be the county seat—Corbinton. Its name was changed to Hillsborough in 1766.[84]

The backwoods outpost quickly became a place of some importance. Placed near an intersection of long-used trading routes and near fording spots on the Eno River, it was already a site for commerce and attracted a population who found proximity to the authorities to be in their interest. Hillsborough was an organizing center for the Regulator insurrection and the spot where Royal Governor William Tryon had six Regulator leaders hanged. During the Revolutionary War, the state legislature met there on occasion and found itself captured en masse in 1781 by the Tory guerilla David Fanning. In 1788, a convention there voted against ratifying the U.S. Constitution (a second convention the next year in Fayetteville changed its mind).

That was young Billy's hometown. His father owned a gristmill—a lucrative occupation—a few miles downriver from town. His birth mother raised the boy on her parents' farm until he was five or six, when Thomas Holden's wife, Sally Nichols, brought Billy into their household and raised him along with the ten children of her and Thomas's own. She didn't tell Thomas ahead of time what she had in mind to do, but family tradition had it that Thomas was pleased.[85]

In the spotty recollections that Holden set down about his childhood, he described typical boys' exploits such as skating, hunting and fights at school. At about the age of ten he became apprentice to Dennis Heartt, who published the *Recorder*, a weekly newspaper that carried such information as commodity prices, classified ads, commentary on state and national affairs and whatever else could be culled from other sources. As an apprentice, Billy served as a menial task boy, sorting and setting type, delivering the paper and running such errands as Heartt required.

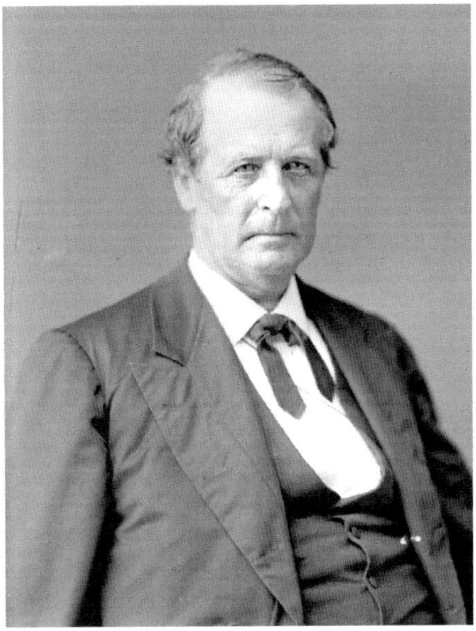

Samuel Ashe met Holden—the newsboy—over muffins; years later, Holden beat him in a race for governor. *Courtesy Library of Congress.*

Biographers have repeated two particular anecdotes from those days that may have affected Holden's adult character or may have simply proven ironic. One Christmas, the entrepreneurial Heartt printed up some seasonal but "very questionable" (as the literary-minded Holden later described it) poetry and sent the boy out to sell it at holiday parties going on around town. Having no luck, young Billy at last tried the residence of a prominent citizen. Festivities were indeed underway there, and the scruffy newsboy found himself ushered in by a servant and presented to the host—who promptly bought his whole stock, gave him a dollar for himself and sent him away with Christmas goodies to eat. Billy's benefactor was William Alexander Graham—with whom he would have less genial dealings in later life.

Another wintry morning when Billy was making his delivery rounds, he was invited into the dining room of a warm and affluent household where a young man home from college was having his breakfast. The lady of the house gave Billy a hot muffin, and while he was savoring the treat he imagined himself living in luxury, reflected on the disparities of the human condition and determined to raise himself in the world to match the scholar across the table. The college boy was named Thomas Ashe, and decades later, Holden would indeed beat Ashe in a race for governor.

Billy Holden lasted as Heartt's apprentice until 1834. On the Fourth of July that year, Heartt, Graham and some other local notables were orators for the town's holiday observance. Billy took the day off, got a whipping for it from the shop foreman and ran away from town. A story goes that the next week, he saw that the *Recorder* carried an ad offering a nickel to anyone who would fetch him back to work. Inspired, he broke into the office and inserted an ad in the next edition that offered the *Recorder* and its editor for sale for fifty cents. Whatever the truth of that, Holden and Heartt made up their differences, Holden worked out his apprenticeship time and, finished, struck out on his own in the newspaper business. Ironically again, his first stop was in Caswell County, where he found work with the *Milton Spectator*. Soon, though, he moved across the Dan River to Danville, Virginia, saw his first writing published and then wandered back to Hillsborough and thought about what to do with himself—clerking in a store, voraciously reading to educate himself and writing occasional items for the *Raleigh Star* newspaper.[86]

Thus encouraged, on October 7, 1836, Holden caught the stagecoach for Raleigh. Ironically again, he traveled in the company of two students from Greensboro's Caldwell Institute, a three-year-old Presbyterian institution that emphasized classical studies and "old-fashioned discipline."[87] The two were William J. Clarke, who would in 1870 command a unit of then governor Holden's militia, and Thomas Sparrow, who would in 1870 make himself Holden's leading adversary.[88]

> *I came to Raleigh in the year 1836, a lad, not quite eighteen years of age, and began work in the old* Raleigh Star *office, still standing, as a typesetter, or compositor. I was not a regular journeyman printer, for I had not learned to lock up forms or do job printing. I was only a very swift compositor. I remained in the* Star *office, boarding in the family of the Editor, the Rev. Thomas J. Lemay, for more than four years. I was a close, hard student of books and men. During the period I read law, mainly at night after the labors of the day were over, and on the 1st day of January, 1841, I obtained license in the County Courts, the Supreme Court consisting then of Chief Justice Ruffin and Judges Gaston and Daniel.*[89]

North Carolina's capital had been a movable feast through the colonial and early post-Revolutionary years, the legislature convening at various places until 1792, when the state authorities settled on the crossroads tavern of one Isaac Hunter as a convivial and convenient site to seat the government. By 1836, the capital had about two thousand residents, a handful of mansions, boardinghouses, hotels, hog pens and a Capitol building under construction—all in all, not very different from the town Holden had just left, but nevertheless a lively place with opportunities for a young man on the make.

Lemay, like Heartt, was a Whig—advocate for the political party formed two years earlier by disaffected Democrats and former Federalists who considered President "King Andrew" Jackson a corrupt, partisan tyrant inimical to the nation's future. Generally speaking, Whigs favored business and industry, in contrast to the agrarian ideal of Thomas Jefferson and his "Democratic Republicans," later just "Republicans" and, still later, "Democrats." Whigs supported banks, protectionist tariffs and internal improvements such as canals, plank roads and, as technology developed, railroads. Their most prominent national figures were the Kentucky U.S. senator Henry Clay, who introduced the term "Whig" to the American political lexicon, and Daniel Webster, of "The Devil and…" fame, from Massachusetts. In North Carolina, the party attracted many powerful figures, among them William Graham and, also from Orange County, U.S. senator Willie P. Mangum and Duncan Cameron, a judge and planter who would own the state's largest plantation by the time of the Civil War.

Holden arrived in Raleigh with seven dollars, a gold watch, a stylish new coat and a job at one of the state's most powerful journals. Starting as a typesetter, he gained Lemay's confidence to the point that the editor let him write editorials supporting states' rights and national expansion into the West. In much later life, Holden recalled the 1830s party distinctions:

> *In a social sense, the Democrats of the State were regarded as no better than the Scalawags of modern times. The Whigs were mainly in the towns and villages, and it was claimed that they possessed a large portion of all the "intelligence and the decency," while the great bulk of the Democrats were, in the eye of society, ignorant and awkward. The Democrats, too, were understood to be opposed to common schools and internal improvements, while the Whigs were the liberals and in favor of both.*[90]

Despite the Whigs' lofty social standing, Holden and the *Star* disdained Jackson's successor, the New York Democrat Martin Van Buren, for his alleged pretensions to aristocracy, and in the 1840 presidential contest the Whigs adopted a log cabin as their emblem and roused the electorate with rallies that borrowed style and volume from summertime camp meetings, as editor Heartt reported in the *Recorder*:

> *The Whigs on Stony Creek deserve great praise for their zeal and activity in the good cause. They came up in strong force to the meeting, numbering (with the recruits who joined them on the road) more than 400, bringing with them a remarkably well constructed log cabin, surmounted with two or three neat banners and other emblems, accompanied with music, and throughout all their movements exhibited a spirit which augurs well for*

the November election. It is supposed that there were present at the meeting not less than ten or twelve hundred persons.[91]

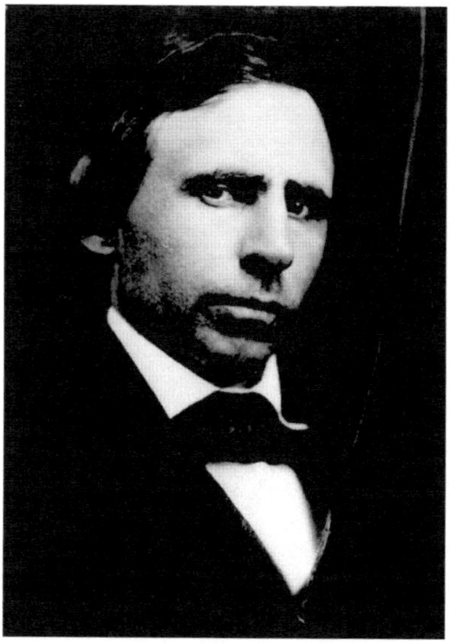

William Woods Holden as a young man. He arrived in Raleigh in 1836 poor, unknown and "very ambitious." *Courtesy the North Carolina State Archives.*

Taking up the practice of law, Holden dove into politics, represented Wake County at a state Whig convention and raised himself to such stature that, in 1842, he could woo and win Ann Young, granddaughter of a well-to-do Raleigh merchant and landowner. That same year, Lemay invited Holden to buy part interest in the *Star*. Holden was interested, but when he tapped some fellow Whigs—Graham, in particular—for a loan, they turned him down. Miffed—or maybe his opinions really had changed—Holden went over to the "awkward and ignorant" side.

Whigs by then in control of North Carolina's government, Democrats were looking to restore their prospects and saw one tool in reviving their party organ, the *North Carolina Standard*. Having seen some ability in their rival Holden, and needing someone both editorially and fiscally competent, they offered him not only the job but also a loan of $2,500 to buy the paper. Holden had made himself so respectable that most of the money came from the State Bank of North Carolina, whose president, Duncan Cameron, may have been a political adversary but considered Holden a good financial risk.[92] It was a risky bet, but Cameron's judgment was sound:

> *My subscription list at the time was eight hundred, and my advertising patronage about two columns. The circulation of the paper was greatly reduced, and business men, especially the Whigs, did not wish to support the organ of the Democratic Party. For six months the subscription list stood still, neither advancing or receding. Meanwhile I had engaged several very able writers who wrote anonymously for the paper, and I had also written the numbers for the paper known as the "Mysteries of Coondom Revealed," which were designed, as they did, to set forward in a ridiculous light the leaders of the Whig Party. It is true I was comparatively a stranger to*

> *my readers and to the people of the State, but at the end of the six months referred to I perceived a sudden and great quickening in my subscription.*[93]

Holden's former associates, now his targets, were not amused, and Holden had left himself open to the charges of opportunism and inconstancy that would follow him the rest of his career. The *Greensboro Patriot*, no friend to Holden later on, commented on his change of party: "Mr. Holden is a very smart young man; but the integrity of a renegade is always more or less doubted." Holden attacked the Raleigh Whigs as a clique that had "for a moment crept up from the dirt to opulence" and began presenting himself as a man of humble origins and the Democratic Party as a champion of the common folk, notwithstanding the fact that many of its members owned large estates and numbers of slaves. Aristocracy, or pretensions thereto, was a sore point in the Vale of Humility, and both parties could actually count within their memberships individuals from across the state's socioeconomic spectrum.

To rally the disorganized Democrats, Holden picked the state finances as an issue and attacked the ruling Whigs for internal improvements, particularly a railroad connecting the Wilmington port with Virginia, which, he claimed, had run up a public debt in the hundreds of thousands of dollars—notwithstanding that such improvements gave many of the state's sturdy yeomen access to outside markets for the first time and that North Carolina's backward economy made it known as the "Rip Van Winkle State." His invective and political senses paid off: by 1850, he had repaid his creditors, bought a house, installed a steam-powered printing press and had $5,000 in the bank. He had been elected to the legislature—judiciously refraining from endorsing himself in his paper—where he supported an $800 appropriation for a turnpike in mountainous Buncombe County in return for a Buncombe legislator's support for a $12,000 appropriation for a fence around the Capitol.

On the state front, Holden campaigned for equal suffrage in electing state senators, as voting in those contests then was limited to persons owning fifty acres or more. On the national front, he vigorously supported annexation of Mexico, though he tried to downplay that issue during the 1846 governor's race since North Carolinians were largely unsympathetic to the war it provoked. Realizing that railroads and turnpikes were popular among the people, in 1848 Holden dropped his former opposition and called for "a bold, a general, and a vigorous system of Internal Improvements." For that, he was labeled an apostate by some of his own party and had a particularly ticklish time in 1850 maintaining friendly relations with the anti-railroad

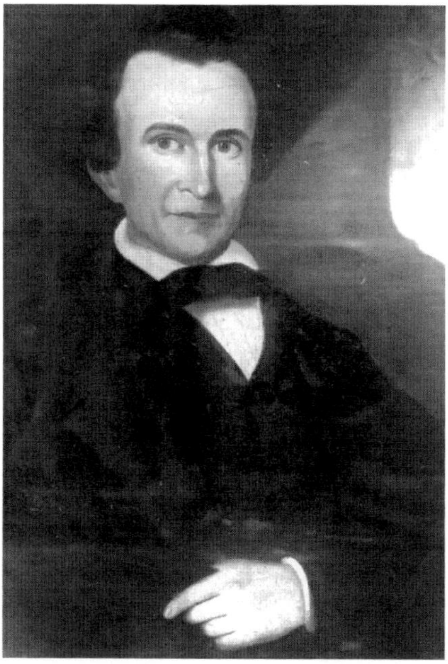

As a candidate for governor in 1850, David S. Reid had an awkward relationship with Holden, the party publicist. *Courtesy the North Carolina State Archives.*

Democratic gubernatorial candidate, David S. Reid.

But Holden was nothing if not politically adept. Heading off an impending party split, he persuaded Reid to remain a candidate and reaped a windfall when the Whig incumbent, Charles Manly, formerly opposing equal (white, male) suffrage, changed his mind with the condition of abolishing the federal provision that counted slaves as three-fifths citizens for representation in the House of Commons. Manly thus set himself against the interests of easterners with large slave populations and made himself look politically desperate to the rest of the state. Holden, in the *Standard*, was quick to capitalize on the gaffe to paint Manly as a demagogue threatening the very basis of Southern influence in Congress at the same time as the issue of slavery's expansion into the new western territories was creating a national crisis. Reid and the Democrats were swept into power in Raleigh, and suddenly slavery and states' rights were dominating all other political questions.

Holden admired the South Carolinian John C. Calhoun, who had championed the rights of states to nullify federal acts and to, as a last resort, withdraw from the Union. Holden saw, in an effort to ban slavery in the territory won from Mexico, an act of aggression toward the South aimed at making abolition the law of the land, and he urged the Southern states to unite in the face of such threat and to meet together for planning their defensive response. He then changed his mind when it became apparent that most North Carolinians were not interested in the proposed Nashville Convention and adopted as the *Standard*'s slogan "The Constitution and the Union of the States—They must be preserved" while still condemning abolitionists like then U.S. senator William Seward and defending slavery's extension into new states.

Waffler or not, renegade or not, Holden emerged from 1850 as a power in a party on the rise and with a contract to handle the state's printing business. Detractors regarded him as the governor de facto, and he did enhance his influence in the next few years of Democratic rule, with appointments to the university's board of trustees, the state board administering money for public schools and several county and state authorities. His wife, Ann, died in 1852; after two years as a widower, he married Louisa Virginia Harrison, of another prominent mercantile and landowning family. She would bear him four children to go along with the four of Ann's, and she made herself a gracious hostess to the numerous people coming to call on her husband. With his home life warm and rewarding, his business prospering as never before and the Whig Party disintegrating from internal splits over slavery, Holden was at a peak of his life. In 1858, he decided to run for governor himself.

Unfortunately for Holden, he had aggravated a party split of the Democrats' own. Duncan McRae, a prominent party man of Cumberland County, came out in late 1857 supporting distribution of federal land to the states. That was a position Holden and the rest of the party leadership had previously opposed, and Holden attacked McRae as an agent of the old Whigs and the new Know-Nothing Party. Holden's charges only encouraged McRae's ambitions to be governor, showed off Holden's tendencies to intemperate language and behavior and made him look like an inside boss indifferent to what the party membership at large thought—the "Pope of Hargett Street," as Holden's opponents styled him. At the party convention, Holden lost the nomination to John W. Ellis. Later that year, with a new legislature due to elect U.S. senators, some of Holden's associates, acting without Holden's knowledge, put his name in the running. Even though Holden declared he wasn't interested in the Senate, many in the party concluded that he was trying to have things both ways, and Holden came out with no seat and was regarded as a figure of disunion even though he strongly backed Ellis and the General Assembly's choices for Senate.

The Democrats retained power in 1858. But in 1859, John Brown, an abolitionist notorious for his bloody guerilla actions in Kansas, led a raid on the Harpers Ferry armory in Virginia. And everything started to change.[94]

BRIGHT LEAVES AND IMPENDING CRISIS

While Billy Holden was realizing his great expectations, back in his home country times went drifting by. The still-vast Orange County had Hillsborough, its seat, and Chapel Hill, its university village, and some crossroads hamlets here and there, but it was dominated by countryside and peppered with small farms that were organized, in the minds of its inhabitants, in terms of "neighborhoods" defined by kinship and marriage relations.[95] Churches provided a bit of society and social cohesion for country folk that helped soothe over the occasional grudge and dispute; country stores and gristmills were also gathering places, the latter a rudimentary industrial base that rose in abundance along the plentiful small streams and rudimentary roads leading from one ford to another.

The country folk raised corn and hogs, primarily, each of which had various uses, from eating fresh to rendering down for lard. Tobacco was another common crop that was raised just enough for home consumption in a pipe, as a chew or for a dip, as snuff. Sometimes a man would spare a twist or two for sale in town, but the old brown leaf was a standard of most every kitchen garden. There were also cows for milk and their products that, like the wheat, oats and rye also typical of Piedmont fields, provided both staples for home consumption and market goods for those who could take the time, or pay the freight, to get them to waterfront towns such as Halifax and Fayetteville, in eastern North Carolina; Lynchburg, on Virginia's upper James River; or Charleston, South Carolina, where the Ashley and Cooper Rivers join to form the Atlantic Ocean. But roads were bad and travel slow—

the fifty-mile trip between Milton, on the Virginia border, and Chapel Hill took two uncomfortable days by coach, assuming the creeks were not too high and the road not too deep in mud. Life on the red clay Piedmont land was tough; the heartland of Rip Van Winkle North Carolina bled population as well as capital. By 1850, one-third of native-born North Carolinians had moved away in hope of finding somewhere better.[96]

Frederick Law Olmsted, the future architect of New York's Central Park and North Carolina's Biltmore Estate, toured the South in 1856 and described the country folk he encountered in Harnett County near Raleigh in dreary terms remarkably like those William Byrd had used 128 years earlier:

> *They are poor, having almost no common property but their own bodies...A family of these people will commonly hire or "squat" and build a little log cabin, so made that it is only a shelter from rain, the sides not being chinked, and having no more furniture or pretension to comfort than is commonly provided a criminal in the cell of a prison. They will cultivate a little corn, and possibly a few roods of potatoes, cow peas and coleworts* [collards? cabbage?]. *They own a few swine, that find their living in the forest; and pretty certainly, also a rifle and dogs and the men ostensibly, occupy most of their time in hunting.*[97]

James Bennitt, in whose Orange County cabin Sherman and Johnston held their meetings, was a more industrious example of plain folks, though how he would have impressed the urbane Olmsted must be left to imagination. By the 1850s, Bennitt (the spelling later changed to "Bennett") had amassed 325 acres on either side of the road between Hillsborough and Raleigh. The Bennitts grew enough corn to sell some and turn some into saleable whiskey, besides what they needed for home use. Typical of the place and time, they raised wheat and vegetables, hogs, cattle and chickens. On the side, James Bennitt made shoes and his wife made clothing—again, some for home use and some for sale, to neighbors as well as passersby on the heavily traveled road a few feet from their front door.[98]

For the Piedmont, though, Caswell County told a different story. It lost population in only one decade, 1830 to 1840, and then only by 492.[99] Another indicator of its difference is its slave population compared with counties to the south. In 1786, that part of Caswell not later set off for Person County had 5,193 inhabitants, 1,076 of whom were black; in 1860, there were 16,215 total, more than half of whom were slaves: 9,355. Orange County had 2,000 slaves in 1790 and 10,000 whites, figures that rose to

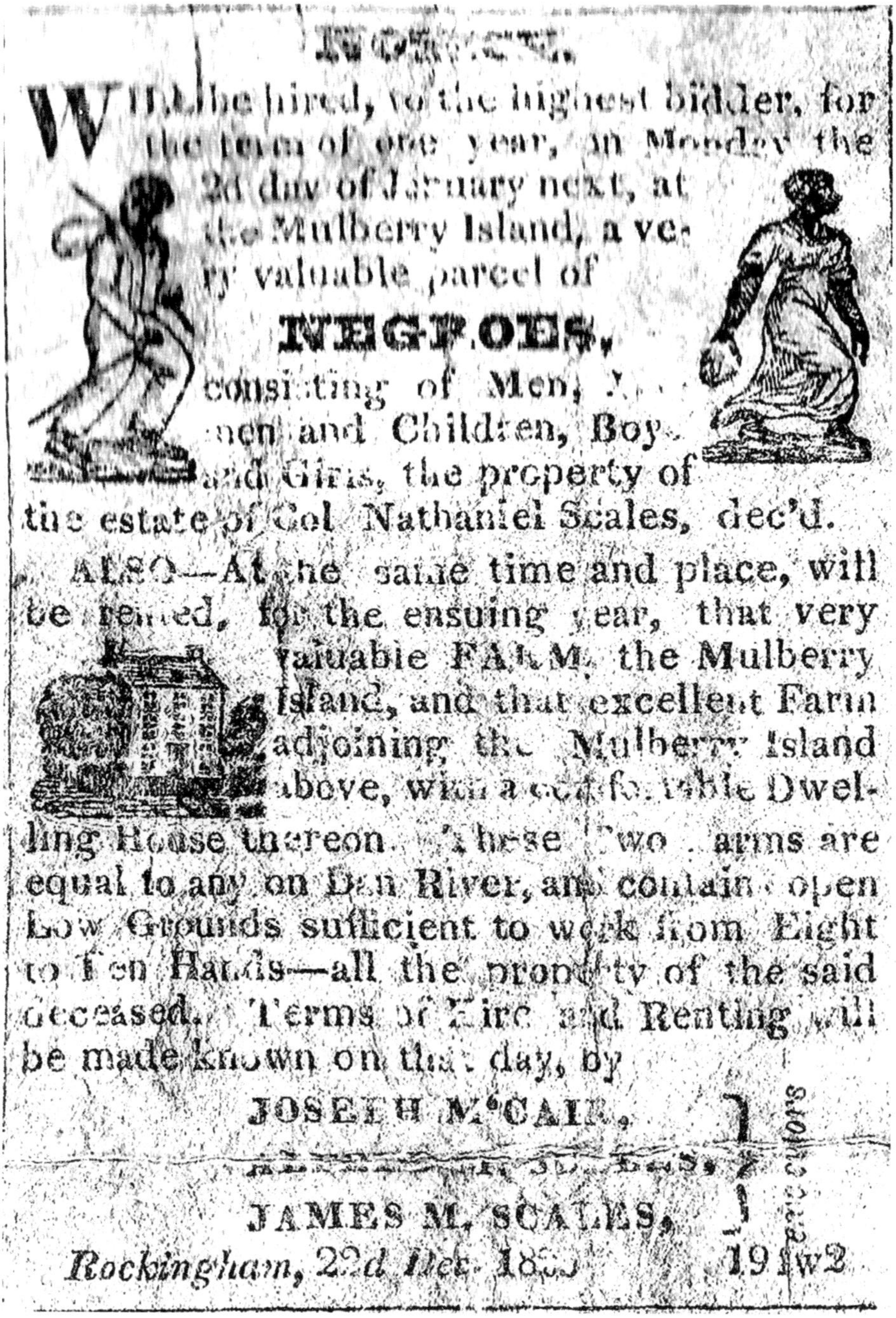
NOTICE.

WILL be hired, to the highest bidder, for the term of one year, on Monday the 2d day of January next, at the Mulberry Island, a very valuable parcel of

NEGROES,

consisting of Men, Women and Children, Boys and Girls, the property of the estate of Col Nathaniel Scales, dec'd.

ALSO—At the same time and place, will be rented, for the ensuing year, that very valuable FARM, the Mulberry Island, and that excellent Farm adjoining the Mulberry Island above, with a comfortable Dwelling House thereon. These Two Farms are equal to any on Dan River, and contain open Low Grounds sufficient to work from Eight to Ten Hands—all the property of the said deceased. Terms of Hire and Renting will be made known on that day, by

JOSEPH M'CAIN,

JAMES M. SCALES,

Rockingham, 22d Dec. 18

19 w2

Newspaper advertisement for a sale of slaves in Caswell County. *Courtesy Caswell County Historical Association.*

5,108 slaves and 11,311 whites in 1860. The western half of Orange County was sliced off to become Alamance County in 1849; in that county, 3,556 slaves represented 29 percent of the 1860 population.[100]

In short, Caswell was a place more typical of the plantation South than its southern neighbors, which in the early America era remained more typical of the old backcountry. With the wide Dan River snaking along its northern edge, Caswell County enjoyed relative ease in reaching the outside world. The North Carolina legislature established a tobacco inspection station at a Caswell County riverside warehouse in 1791, and the Virginia legislature authorized a tobacco market at Danville, just across the state line, in 1793. Such fortune, along with sandy loam instead of the Piedmont's typical clay soil, led Caswell to become one of the state's largest, wealthiest and most influential counties of the antebellum era.

The county had been sliced off from Orange in 1777, after years of its residents complaining that Hillsborough was too far off and hard to get to when they had to transact official business. The first county seat was Leasburg, named for a pioneer family of the region that prospered and multiplied with the county's fortunes; eleven Leas had signed a petition for the county in 1771,[101] and upon the selection of his namesake site, a hometown journalist, Joshua Lea, observed, "Neighbors around Leasburg welcome heartily the prospect of conducting official business at a place not far from their homes and the prospect of a better economy which will accompany the setting up of a center of government nearby."[102]

It was not to be, for in 1792 the legislature harkened to the inhabitants of eastern Caswell County, who felt Leasburg was too difficult of access to suit them and wanted a county of their own. Leasburg was actually near the middle of the original Caswell County; with the divide, it was almost at the county line. Surveyors were appointed to find the precise center of the diminished Caswell, and there they established Caswell Courthouse, later to be renamed Yanceyville. Within twenty years, a town had grown up around the courthouse that boasted two taverns, two dry goods stores, more than a dozen homes, blacksmiths, carriage makers, silversmiths, physicians, preachers and, of course, lawyers.[103]

Besides Leasburg and Caswell Courthouse, the Dan River town of Milton began after the legislature approved a second inspection station for tobacco, this one for flour as well. Milton grew with commerce rather than government, supported by a multitude of mills that in turn supported a twenty-room hotel, the county's first newspaper, the Milton Female Academy and a leisure class devoted to horse racing, cards and lavish partying.[104] One of the town's prominent citizens was Romulus Saunders—legislator, congressman, American minister to Spain and trustee of the University of North Carolina in spite of the fact that he had been kicked out of the school for "firing a pistol in the College and throwing a rock at the faculty."[105] Another was Thomas Day, a free, well-educated black cabinetmaker whose work was prized by the state's leading families and graced the hall of the university's literary societies. Day himself became prominent enough that, when he married a black woman in Virginia, the North Carolina legislature passed a special act allowing Day to bring his bride into the state—travel by even free African Americans having been restricted to prevent their influence on slaves. Day owned land, slaves and a sizable interest in the local bank, and his family's pew was in the front row at the Milton Presbyterian Church.

Day was a special case. Central North Carolina had some hundreds of free blacks, most of them small farmers like their white neighbors, who lived on scattered holdings among the whites with no pattern of race-based settlement. Indicating a pattern of fear and discrimination, though, the legislature passed laws forbidding free blacks, or slaves, from holding prayer meetings or preaching, in reaction to the 1831 Virginia insurrection led by the slave preacher Nat Turner, which set off a panic in Raleigh when news arrived and set students at the university mobilizing to defend Chapel Hill.[106]

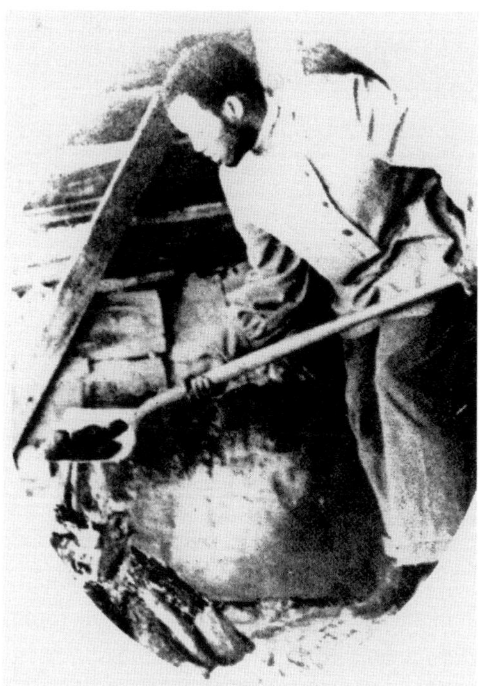

Stephen Slade discovered the highly profitable effect of heat on tobacco leaves as a Caswell County slave. *Courtesy Duke Homestead State Historic Site.*

Free blacks, though, were vastly outnumbered by slaves, and it was one of those slaves who brought the land a bonanza. He was Stephen, a slave on the Caswell plantation of Abisha Slade. Though just eighteen, Stephen was the plantation blacksmith, but when tobacco harvest season came, he, like every other resident of a tobacco farm, was pressed into duty tending the precious leaves. One evening in 1839, Stephen was posted to mind the curing fires—a vital job, because the temperature needed to be kept steady for the crop to turn out right, but boring nonetheless. Stephen drifted off to sleep, and when he woke, he discovered, to his consternation, that the curing fire had just about burned out.

Knowing that he was about to be in trouble, Stephen thought quickly. He sped to his smithy, scooped up a load of charcoal, ran back and dumped it on what remained of the fire. The curing fire burst back to life with a rush of heat, and as he watched, Stephen saw the tobacco turning out, not the customary brown, but a glorious shade of golden yellow. Many years later, he told an interviewer: "To tell the truth about it, 'twas an accident. I commenced to cure [the tobacco] and it commenced to get yallow. It kep' on yallowin' and kep' on yallowin' and kep' on yallowin' twell it got clar up…It looked so purty. I kept making it yallow and when it was cured it was 'musement for folks to come and see it."[107]

No one had ever seen tobacco like it. Not only was it pretty, but the bright leaf—as it became known—also smoked mild and pleasing. Stephen—or rather, his owner—had six hundred pounds of it, and when it went to market in Danville, it brought forty dollars per hundred pounds when the going rate was ten.

Abisha Slade and his brothers William and Elias began experimenting with heat and tobacco and refined a curing method that consistently turned out high-quality, golden leaves that raised growers' profit margins almost exponentially. Also, the particular variety of tobacco that produced the best bright leaf thrived in infertile soils, and a farmer with only his family and maybe a hired hand or leased slave or two could produce enough to be worth hauling to market. The Slades became veritable evangelists for bright leaf tobacco and spread its cash crop culture not only across the established belt along the Dan-Roanoke River system along the Virginia–North Carolina line but also into areas such as Orange and recently created Alamance (sectioned from Orange) Counties, where it had been only a household staple.

In 1860, Alamance County was growing thirty-five times as much tobacco as it had a decade before. Statewide, North Carolina had produced fewer than 5 million pounds of tobacco in 1830; by 1850, the total was up to 12 million, and it almost tripled in the next decade. Caswell County had the state's third-largest tobacco crop in 1860, with 4.6 million pounds; Orange County was number eight, with 1.16 million.[108]

Yellow leaves weren't the only factor in the Piedmont's tobacco boom. The North Carolina Railroad, completed in 1856, ran through the state's

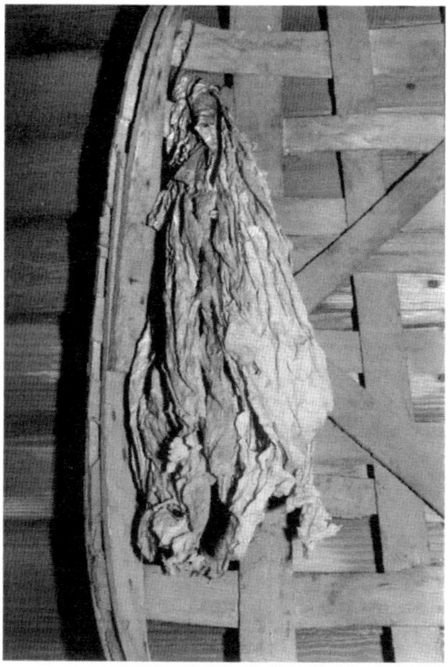

Tobacco was the basis of Caswell County prosperity, with a combination of local markets, proper soil and bright yellow leaves. *Author's photo.*

midsection. From Charlotte, a trade crossroads near the South Carolina border, the line arced north and east through Salisbury, Greensboro, Graham, Hillsborough, Raleigh and on to Goldsboro, where it met the Wilmington and Weldon Railroad leading to Virginia and the coast. Old towns grew as market centers and new ones formed around lonely depots. Farmers suddenly had fast and cheap access to ports and markets as trains went one way and to manufactured goods from up north and abroad as the trains came back the other. While twenty North Carolina counties could have been considered to have market economies in 1850, there were forty-eight—more than half the state—by the time South Carolina seceded from the Union.[109]

North Carolina was joining the Industrial Revolution that had come to the North a few decades earlier. Some areas of the state were cotton country, and as the supply of land for expanding cotton culture ran out, growers realized the alternative opportunity in processing their own crop instead of shipping it off to New England or Britain. The state's first cotton mill opened in 1815, but it was not until the 1840s that it began to boom, along the North Carolina Railroad's right of way and other Piedmont locations where the same fast-running streams that were already powering gristmills could be harnessed to run spinning wheels and looms. Orange County's first mill began operation in 1832; by 1840, there were eight, all in the portion that became Alamance, and four more by 1849, including the aptly named Orange Factory in the east.

Cotton mills and cotton culture were symbiotic. In 1820, North Carolina produced the equivalent of about 8,000 480-pound bales (480 pounds was not adopted as the standard "bale" until the 1880s); in 1860, the total was 145,514. Tobacco was likewise bullish: in 1840, the state had about sixty "manufactories" where cured leaf was processed for smoking, dipping or chewing; in 1850, there were eighty-one, nine of them in Caswell County;

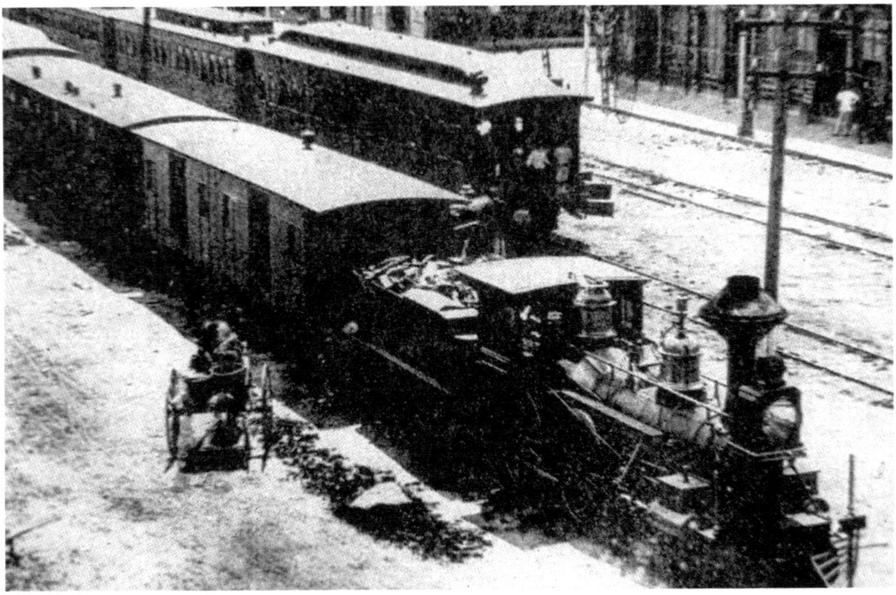

North Carolina Railroad yard at Goldsboro. Completed in 1855, the railroad connected the isolated Piedmont with markets and new ideas. *Courtesy the North Carolina State Archives.*

ten years later, there were ninety-seven, with eleven in Caswell, four in Alamance and two in Orange.[110]

Rip Van Winkle was roused with the clank of machines and the hiss of steam, and whether many small farmers, crossroad storekeepers or self-satisfied plantation masters recognized it, their world was undergoing the same making-over as the New Englander Henry David Thoreau commented on in *Walden*:

> *The startings and arrivals of the cars are now the epochs in the village day. They go and come with such regularity and precision, and their whistle can be heard so far, that the farmers set their clocks by them, and thus one well-conducted institution regulates a whole country. Have not men improved somewhat in punctuality since the railroad was invented? Do they not talk and think faster in the depot than they did in the stage-office? There is something electrifying in the atmosphere of the former place... To do things "railroad fashion" is now the byword.*[111]

It can't be doubted that North Carolinians felt some of that existential angst as their age-old rhythms and horizons were made obsolete, but there was greater angst rising as reports of abolitionist conspiracies appeared in their local news and talk of leaving the Union surfaced in their election-season rallies. Small wonder that, even in major slave-owning counties such as Caswell, the politicians counseled calm and stability and keeping the status quo at the same time that they resented what they felt as attacks on their home country and its rights under the Constitution.[112]

For his part, editor William Holden was worried when the John Brown raid received favorable comment in the North and some of Brown's fellow travelers called for more armed uprisings. The new party of free labor and small business taking shape in the mid-1850s was the "black Republicans" to Holden and others. The *Standard* blamed "their doctrines" for encouraging Brown's action. Holden suggested that it would be a blessing all around if "about one thousand of the prominent abolitionists could be hanged by the neck until they were dead" and warned of dire consequences if level heads failed to check the extremists: "Who can penetrate the gathering gloom before us? Let the South be ready for any emergency. Let North Carolina be ready. Let her be put on a war footing at the next session of the Legislature, whatever may be the result of the [presidential] contest of 1860."[113]

At the same time, Holden admonished slave owners to keep firm hands on their human capital, lest it be swayed to rebellion, and regarded free blacks as a dangerous example to slaves and an idle, improvident drain on the economy to boot.[114]

To compound his difficulties, Whigs and Know-Nothings had reorganized as the Opposition Party for the August 1860 governor's race and adopted populist tax reform as their cause—in particular, an ad valorem tax on property, including slaves. Knowing that a stand either way would alienate a lot of his fellow Democrats, Holden published articles pro and con, but his attempted neutrality actually turned many on both sides against him. When Holden finally came out in favor of the tax at the party's state convention, the delegates voted to set the party platform against it. Holden began describing the Whig proposal as "cunningly devised fables" while downplaying the state election in relation to the national one: "Upon its result will depend the existence of the Union, the safety of our property, and it may be the lives of our families and the destinies of unborn generations."[115]

Holden needn't have been much concerned about the state anyway, since the Democrat Ellis comfortably whipped the Whig John Pool (the same gentleman who would be turned away from the U.S. Senate five years later) and his party won control in the General Assembly. His home county, though, elected a pro–ad valorem Democrat to the legislature, making

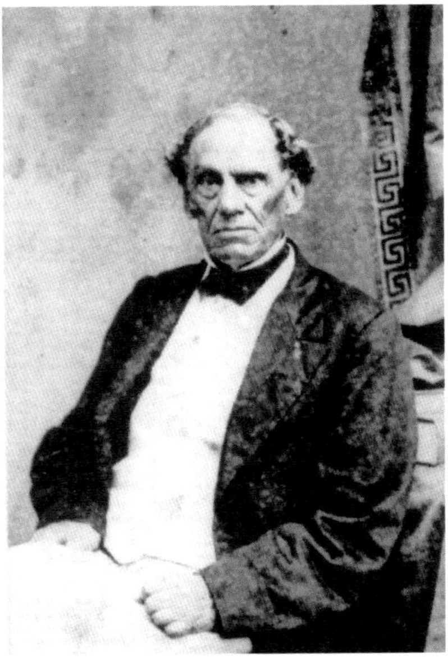

Bedford Brown was one of Caswell County's grand old men of politics. His loss of a state senate race to John W. Stephens angered home folks. *Courtesy Caswell County Historical Association.*

Holden look as if the Pope of Hargett Street was losing his grip. To show that he was still appreciated, the Democrats did make Holden a delegate to the national convention—where the editor who had warned of war learned what he was talking about.

Of all places to hold a national convention in the tense atmosphere of early 1860, the Democrats picked Charleston—home of the South's hottest fire-breathers, where great crowds assembled to have their dander raised by orators fulminating against the Union and all those who counseled moderation when honor was at stake and demanded passion in its defense. Bedford Brown, one of the caution counselors from Caswell County, heard himself denounced. Holden, shaken at what he saw let loose, got his backbone up and rallied his fellow North Carolinians to stand firm against disintegrating the Union. The convention, in chaos, adjourned without picking a presidential nominee and scheduled a second get-together later on, in calmer Baltimore.

There, though, the party split again, the main issue being the federal government's protection of slavery in the western territories. The Deep South demanded it, the Upper South was not so adamant, but after the Democrats divided into a mainstream wing behind Stephen A. Douglas of Illinois and a "Southern Rights" wing behind John C. Breckinridge of Kentucky, most of the North Carolina party stalwarts, including Ellis, adopted the hard line and left Holden, worried that the split would only make a black Republican's election more likely, out in the cold.

The *Standard* would brook no infringement of Southern states' rights but warned of "strife, civil and servile war, murder, arson, pillage, robbery, and fire and blood" if war broke out, all leading to debt, taxes and, just maybe, even military dictatorship. "There is no good cause *now* for dissolving the Union," Holden wrote. "The cause may arise, but let us not hasten to make it or meet it."[116]

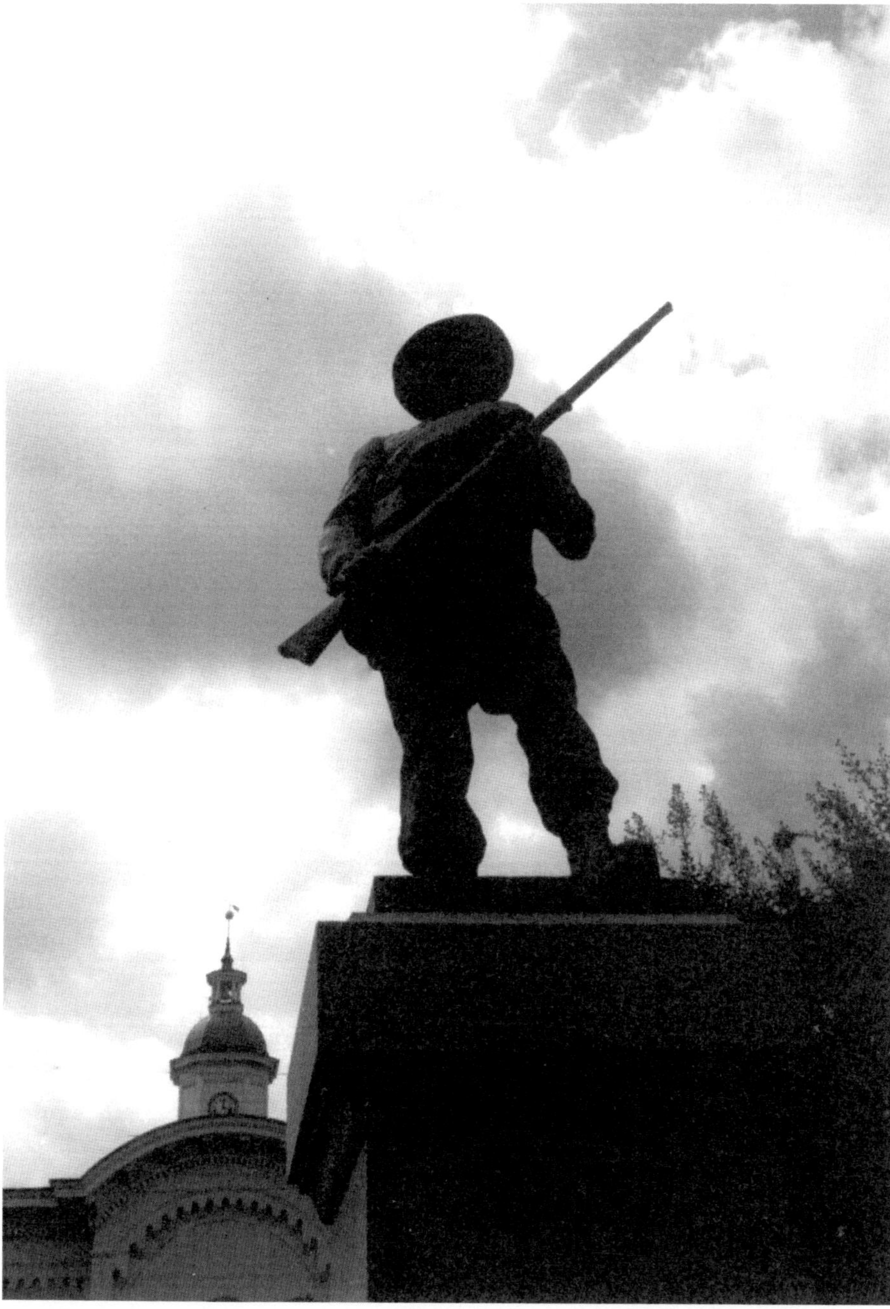

A Confederate sentry stands watch in front of the Caswell County Courthouse where "Chicken" Stephens was murdered. *Author's photo.*

As Holden feared, the Republican Abraham Lincoln won the presidency; but most North Carolinians—particularly old Whigs, many of whom Holden had vilified for years—were with him in preferring to wait on events rather than rushing to secede, as South Carolina did in December. That wasn't enough to keep the Democrats from kicking Holden out of his job as printer to the state, and Holden responded by going after the secessionists in his own party with print and ink, as well as affirming that remaining in the Union was consistent with true Democratic values such as states' rights, strict constructionism in interpreting the Constitution and opposition to the wealthy and aristocratic.

Holden hadn't completely lost his touch. In February 1861, North Carolina voted against holding a state convention to consider secession. In Wake County, the vote went Holden's way, three to one. But Lincoln's actual assumption of the presidency in March, with his inaugural comment that he intended to maintain a military presence in the departed Deep South states, was enough to depress and frighten many others. A North Carolina branch of the Southern Rights Party formed in Goldsboro, where the town newspaper labeled Holden a Lincoln ally. Holden called secessionists the tools of oligarchy who hated Lincoln not because of his policies but because he had split rails with his own hands; and he reported how, in the budding Confederacy, individual liberties were being snuffed out in the name of patriotism and military expedience.[117]

It was the same theme that Holden would carry into and through the war with his attacks on the Confederate government in Richmond and its friends in Raleigh. No matter—in April 1861, Lincoln called for troops to put the South Carolina Rebels down after they forced the Union garrison out of Fort Sumter. North Carolina convened and voted itself out of the United States.

North Carolina's own historians, when discussing the War Between the States, invariably invoke the state's hesitance in seceding; its pro-Union multitudes; its yeoman character in contrast with the Georgians and Mississippians who owned thousands of slaves and tens of thousands of acres; and the fact that it was the last state to join the Confederacy. Only then do they admit that North Carolina sent more men to the Confederate colors, and took more casualties, than any other state. The first Rebel soldier to fall in combat was a North Carolinian, Henry Wyatt of Edgecombe County, and North Carolina units were among those that broke the Union line on Gettysburg's Cemetery Hill to achieve the Confederacy's high-water mark. A well-known state slogan declares, "First at Bethel, farthest at Gettysburg, last [to stack arms] at Appomattox." It was also a North Carolina trooper who shot the Southern hero Stonewall Jackson by mistake, but that's another story.

THE BLACK REPUBLICAN

By the time William Holden gave up the keys to the governor's office in December 1865, it was clear that power in Washington—hence, power over North Carolina—had shifted. Holden took a month's vacation before resuming his newspaper trade and concluding that the Worth administration was putting old Confederates back in power and losing interest in rejoining the United States, at the same time that Andrew Johnson's authority was evaporating and that of the Republican Radicals solidifying.

Tossing down his gauntlet again, he wrote:

> *True Unionists are depressed at the prospect before them, and feel they have a right to look to Washington for sympathy and for such practicable aid as will enable them to put the enemies of the Union where they ought to be—under their feet. And we now give notice that we have commenced this warfare on traitors, not without having counted the cost, and we intend to continue it until they are driven from every office of importance in the State. Nothing shall divert us from our purpose.*[118]

Not even if it meant making common cause with the black Republicans he had blamed for fomenting trouble and the abolitionists whose hanging he had recommended just a few years earlier. When Johnson offered him the job of ambassador to San Salvador, Holden's appointment failed to win congressional approval. Johnson had never made his friend Holden take the loyalty oath required of every other postwar Southern official, even though Holden had served in the home guard, as state printer and as adviser to Governor Vance during the Confederacy. In Johnson's gesture, Holden might have suspected a trick by Worth and his Democrats meant to get him out of their way in North Carolina, but he went to Washington anyway to press his case—and to tell Johnson dark stories of what Worth was up to and hint at the president's removing Worth and putting Holden back in the job.[119]

Johnson would have none of that, and a disappointed Holden went home to advocate for the new state constitution that the convention had drafted after reconvening in February. Governor Worth joined Holden in endorsing the document, but when the state's voters rejected it, Holden concluded that Worth, Graham and their cohorts were determined to block any social change or threat to what political establishment existed. To get the state back into the Union, there was only one thing to do. In Washington, Holden had met with the radical Republican senators Thaddeus Stevens and Charles Sumner, informing them of the precarious situation down home, and on September 20, 1866, with Holden as chairman, twenty representatives of a handful[120] of counties met in Raleigh to organize a new state party of "unmistakable loyal men."

Rather than really organizing, though, the loyal men just adopted resolutions, including one that called for the legislature to ratify the Fourteenth Amendment, guaranteeing full citizenship and civil rights to "all persons born or naturalized in the United States" and barring any state from denying equal protection of the law or depriving any person of life, liberty or property without due process. Holden, in an address to the convention, claimed that the amendment would, nevertheless, leave the matter of blacks' voting rights up to the states.[121]

The Union Party meeting did nominate a candidate for governor in that fall's election to fill the office for a full term—the former Whig Alfred Dockery of Richmond County in the cotton belt along the South Carolina line—but Dockery overlooked the honor. He said the group that had met was too small to be representative of citizens' will, and there weren't but thirty days to go before the election—hardly time to mount an effective campaign. Dockery did get more than ten thousand votes, but Worth got more than thirty-four thousand and won in a walk. Hardly discouraged, Holden and his new friend in Greensboro, Albion Tourgee, began marshaling their allies and asking their friends in Congress to protect them from "Rebel persecution."

Others no doubt read the situation differently. Addressing the legislature on January 19, 1866, Worth expressed his regret that Congress had refused to seat North Carolina's elected representatives and said:

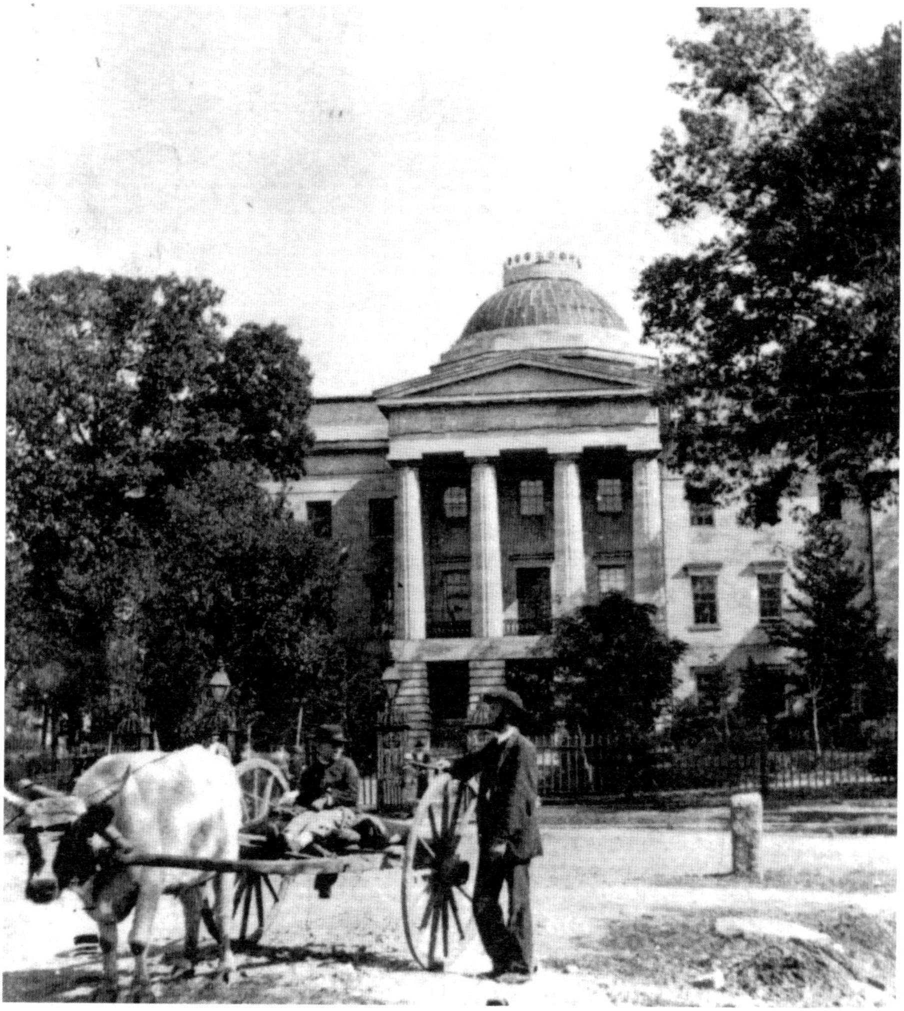

An ox cart in the street in front of North Carolina's Capitol building in the 1800s. *Courtesy the North Carolina State Archives.*

> *I pray God a returning sense of patriotism and justice will ere long correct the prejudices of the time, and carry out the wise system so successfully begun and perfected so far as depended on the Executive authority, for the restoration of the States, of a constitutional and harmonious Union, and that He will inspire all of us with the wisdom and disposition to do right.*[122]

Robert Watson Winston, then a boy on his family's plantation in Bertie County, in the east, described his well-to-do parents as passionate Whigs, and Worth as a "sturdy, long-headed old Quaker" in his 1937 autobiography *It's a Far Cry*. He recalled the early postwar years as an "era of partial good feeling":

> *The Whigs were mistaken in branding all of their Democratic opponents as disunionists…I was brought up to conclude, with Jonathan Worth, that the fire-eaters of the South and the fanatics of the North were guilty of the most wicked, and most useless war ever waged. In truth, just as soon as hostilities ended, North Carolina, as I can bear witness, was thoroughly reconstructed and original secessionists dared not raise their heads…*
>
> *So bitter was the feeling toward the Democratic party that it changed its name and became the Conservative party. But not even this change could entice dyed-in-the-wool Unionists to affiliate with the legatee of the lately deceased secession Democracy. Father's old friend and neighbor, Andrew Craig, a Baptist preacher of force and independence, and the father of Governor Locke Craig, became an out-and-out Republican.*[123]

"Disunion" may not have been as pervasive a sentiment as Holden, Tourgee and Co. claimed, but neither had the state been "thoroughly reconstructed" in April 1865. The state legislature demonstrated that, and particularly riled the Northern Radicals, when it—following the example of other formerly rebellious states—enacted a "black code" to specify what emancipation meant for the state's freedmen.

North Carolina's code, approved in January 1866, declared persons of color, hitherto "aliens through the disability of slavery," to be competent witnesses in legal cases involving other people of color; they might testify in cases where whites were involved upon the parties' consent. The code recognized marriages between former slaves but forbade marriage between black and white; and specified fine and prison as punishment for a white man guilty of rape but death for a black man who committed the same crime. The latter provision was subsequently removed, and as black codes went it was relatively liberal, but the damage had been done.[124] The code, along with selective use of vagrancy laws, led Freedmen's Bureau official Clinton Cilley to conclude that it was intended "to impress thoroughly on the blacks that they are inferior, and must be kept so by law."[125]

Worth claimed that the code was intended to deter vagrancy and crime, and freedmen could enjoy the same civil rights as any other citizen. He also recognized that any restrictions on African Americans' liberty should be moderate, to avoid giving cause for the "odious" Freedmen's Bureau to intervene in the state's business and entrench itself deeper in the state. But the *Raleigh Sentinel*, mouthpiece for the administration, adopted the slogan "For the Constitution of the United States, as it is, and the Union as it Was. No further Amendments"—a direct shot at the Fourteenth.[126]

Conducting his campaign primarily through letters to his supporters, Worth came out against the amendment. Conservatives, née Democrats, considered it the Radicals' wedge for intruding into the South, opening the way for black suffrage. The governor wrote, "No full-blooded North Carolinian will humiliate and degrade himself by favoring this amendment, whatever may be the consequence of refusing to ratify it," and some like-minded individuals thought it better to remain a mere territory than to gain statehood by appeasing the Washington crowd. As for Holden the Republican organizer, he was dubbed an "utterly unscrupulous Radical," a "mortal enemy" to the South.[127]

The amendment was, if not gasoline, at least kerosene applied to a hotbed of nerves and sensitivities already past the kindling point all around. Reaction to its proposal, and its defeat in Southern legislatures, indicates the degree to which emotions were overwhelming pragmatism, much as they had in the years leading up to Fort Sumter. To the Radicals, its rejection was one more proof of Southern intransigence—the generals may have surrendered, but hearts and minds remained defiantly rebellious, and only harsh and punitive measures would drive the Confederates to true submission and repentance. After North Carolina voted the amendment down—forty-five to one in the state senate and ninety-three to ten in the commons—U.S. Grant made a prescient observation: "If the Southern States had accepted the amendment instead of rejecting it so hastily, they would have been admitted by Congress [back into the Union] in December, but now I think they will have to take the amendment, and manhood [including black] suffrage. Congress will insist upon it."[128]

For the freedmen, legal recognition of their civil rights was an overdue gesture from a North that, many had reason to feel, had let them down and did not deserve the trust of people left at liberty but almost helpless among their former masters and other whites who had considered them inferiors before and now regarded them as the cause of all their misery. Some blacks, destitute as winter came on, cursed the liberators who had, in many cases, ransacked their homes and robbed them of what little they had, the same as they had done to the unfortunate whites along Sherman's route. Tourgee's

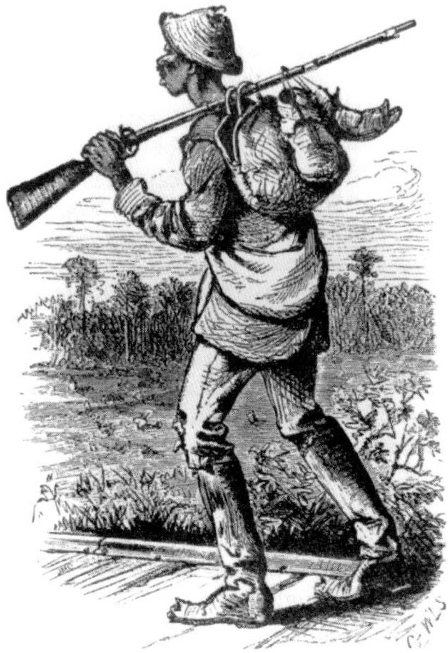

After the Civil War, many slaves went off seeking relatives and opportunity or just to travel freely. Alarmed whites countered with vagrancy laws. *Courtesy the North Carolina State Archives.*

farm was a rare case. More often, the contract employment that freedmen found available was little better than slavery. As one freedman put it, the Yankees had left the former slaves without "any chance to live for ourselves" and forced to "depend on the Southern white man for work, food and clothing."[129] Some resisted, as the *New York Times* reported: "In portions of North Carolina they refuse to work for $15 a month and rations, being desirous of farming on shares without a manager over them. This feeling prevails among them throughout that State, and they utterly refuse to bind themselves on any conditions."[130]

Even though the alternative may have been near-starvation. Whites, though, seeing the freedmen through old prejudice and new anger, took freedmen's unwillingness to bind themselves as proof of their laziness and good reason for enforcing the vagrancy laws against them. The Freedmen's Bureau was in place to hand out food and clothing, rudimentary education and mediation in labor disputes. But everything it did to help the blacks at the same time aggravated white attitudes.

For Southern whites, the Washington government's rejection of the Sherman-Johnston terms was a sign that the North meant to continue the war, just in a different manner. Women who had been left to manage as they could while their menfolk were away, and who had suffered even more at Northern hands than the soldiers, had an informed fear and a particular virulence. Elizabeth Collier, who had fled her home in Goldsboro as Sherman approached, apprehended "disgrace and degradation in store for us," and Catherine Edmondston, the plantation wife who would call Holden "the base-born bastard," wrote of "Yankee power and the Yankee brutality" and of racial animosities, leading inevitably to "rapine and murder" by blacks and "stern retribution" by whites.[131]

Already, in the weeks just after Johnston and Sherman met, Cornelia Phillips Spencer recorded that, in the country around Chapel Hill, marauding Yankees were "ransacking houses, plundering fields, stealing whatever they could and then wasting much of it, giving it to negroes and prostitutes."[132] Wandering freedmen, looking for work, kinfolk or just farther horizons, "stole everything they could get their hands on." Not long after classes resumed at the university in August, a racial brawl left heads and arms broken, and an ex-Confederate soldier whipped a black woman who "maligned a Southern lady."[133]

That was mild. About that same time, a freedman and a former Southern soldier got into a fight in Pittsboro, about twenty miles south of Chapel Hill. The freedman was arrested and sentenced to thirty-nine lashes, administered in three sessions of thirteen lashes each. The sheriff hoped that such painful and ignominious punishment would satiate white bloodlust before a lynch mob took over. Nevertheless, the freedman's opponent tried to pistol-whip the convict while he was still in chains. The Freedmen's Bureau investigated but could never learn the ex-Confederate's identity.[134]

Violence only intensified as time went by. From June 15 through July 15, 1866, the bureau recorded twelve "outrages" in North Carolina, including assault, rape, shooting, whipping and eight homes burned. In August, it learned of twenty more such incidents.[135] At a freedmen's convention in October 1866, some delegates reported peaceful relations between the races at home, or qualified the unpleasantness; for example, Edmund Bird of Alamance County said that prejudice against his people was "only entertained by the lower and ignorant class of whites, whilst the intelligent and better classes are disposed to help the negro." Just as many had the opposite experience:

> *Calvin MacCray, of Richmond* [County] *states...people residing in Richmond county are most shamefully treated by the whites. Their money and fire arms are taken from them under the pretext that it is an order issued for them to take these things away, and colored laborers are most cruelly whipped on plantations...*
>
> *Mr. Hubbard Little, of Montgomery...spoke well of the whites in general but we were pained to hear from him that a colored man was shot and instantly killed for trespassing on the premises of a white person, and he further states that his people are in a most deplorable condition, they having no colored church or school house...*
>
> *Mr. C. Harrel's, of Bertie, discourse was one series of complaint, stating that colored men were cheated out of their labor, children were taken*

> *and bound without the consent or consultation of their parents, no schools for colored persons…*
>
> *Mr. Thos. Hawking, of Burke, in his address states that two colored persons have recently been shot down, and the whites entertain a feeling of prejudice and animosity toward blacks…*
>
> *Mr. Louis Heagie, of Forsyth, stated that the mass of colored people in that county were in an abject state of poverty.*

A resolution began: "WHERAS…outrages are being committed, such as killing, shooting, and robbing the unprotected people, for the most trivial offence, and, in many instances, for no offence at all; and, whereas, those criminals who permit these fiendish outrages are allowed to roam freely at large without being arrested."

The freedmen invited William A. Graham to their convention. The venerable politician begged off attending but sent his respects and his by-your-bootstraps advice:

> *In the present situation of the colored people, the first object of every one should be to obtain an honest livelihood for himself and his family, by labor. The idle will be sure to become vicious, lose the confidence and respect of the community—probably fall into crime, and subject themselves to the punishment of the law. Next to being industrious, they should be frugal—save and lay up what they earn, and when they become able, buy land or other property, and thus advance in the scale of life. Both parents and children who are able to do useful work, should apply themselves to it, until something shall in this way be accumulated. Then they will have the means and time to attend the schools and improve their time. If both objects can be effected at the same time, it will be so much the better. You will perceive that, in my opinion, instruction in morals and virtue, and the religious training derived from hearing the Gospel preached, and in Sunday schools, are more necessary to your people, at present than the knowledge of letters and books.*

This was probably not advice that delegates were inclined to hear again—and again. Governor Worth had similar things to say when he appeared in person. The minutes recorded: "He urges the people to acquire habits of industry, sobriety and honesty. He also spoke touchingly on the late war; of the present position and feelings of the most intelligent classes of both races, and in conclusion strongly urges upon them the importance of acquiring knowledge and wealth."

On the convention's last morning, it was William Holden's turn to speak. The former provisional governor began by reminding the freedmen that they had in fact come far: if, two years earlier, anyone had predicted that North Carolina black people would be free, holding a convention of their own and receiving the governor, "that person would have been regarded as wanting in sanity." He went on to emphasize that the races were interdependent—that blacks should cultivate whites' friendship and that whites' best interest lay in just dealings with the blacks. But again, he stressed learning and labor; he advised against public gatherings, "all temptations to idleness and dissipation" and getting involved in politics, for that was "a weariness to the flesh" for whites.

Nevertheless, the convention sent a message to North Carolina:

> *We, the colored People of North-Carolina…deem it our duty to present to you our grievances, our sufferings and the outrages heaped upon us, because of our helpless and disqualified position for self-defence, resulting, as we think we can prove, from no greater cause than our long and unjust political disfranchisement…*
>
> *FELLOW-CITIZENS: You have taught us one good thing, which we cannot forget. It is this: "That all men are born free and equal, and that they are endowed by their Creator with inalienable rights. That among these are life, liberty and the pursuit of happiness. That to secure these rights, governments are instituted among men, deriving their just powers from the consent of the governed," &c.*
>
> *FELLOW-CITIZENS: Can we look to you for protection or not, to shield us from the murderous hand? Oh, humanity, where is thy blush? Our defenceless wives and children, fathers, sons and brothers are beaten with clubs, robbed, shot and killed, in various localities, and the authorities regard it not. We beg you as white men in authority to shield our defenceless heads, and guard our little homes. We appeal to your religion and humanity. We claim by merit the right of suffrage, and ask it at your hands. We believe the day has come, when black men have rights which white men are bound to respect. We intend to live and die on the soil which gave us birth. Oh, North-Carolina, the land of our birth, with all thy faults we love thee still. Will you, oh! Will you treat us as human beings, with all our rights? It is all we ask.*

Further, attendees at the convention established the Equal Rights League, an organization "to secure, by political and moral means, as far as may

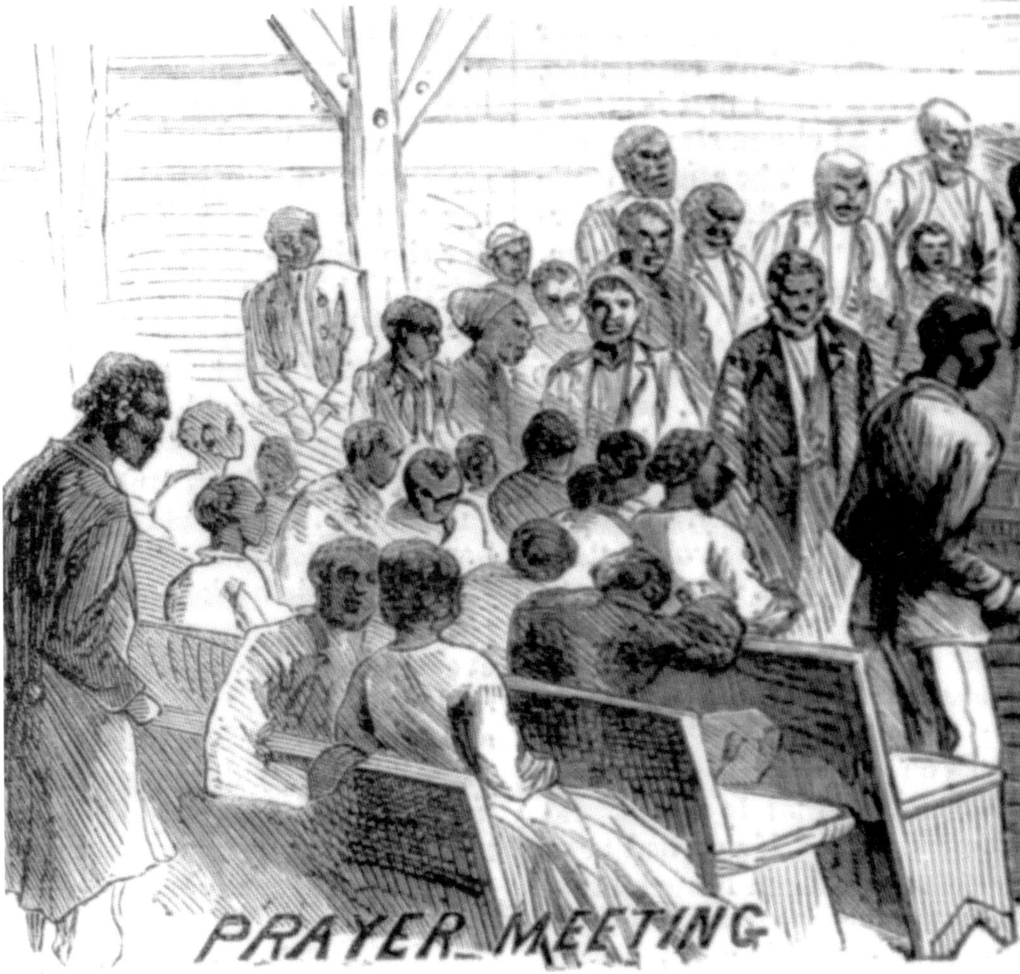

A black prayer meeting during Reconstruction. Forming congregations of their own was one of the first ways freedmen exercised their new liberty. *Courtesy the North Carolina State Archives.*

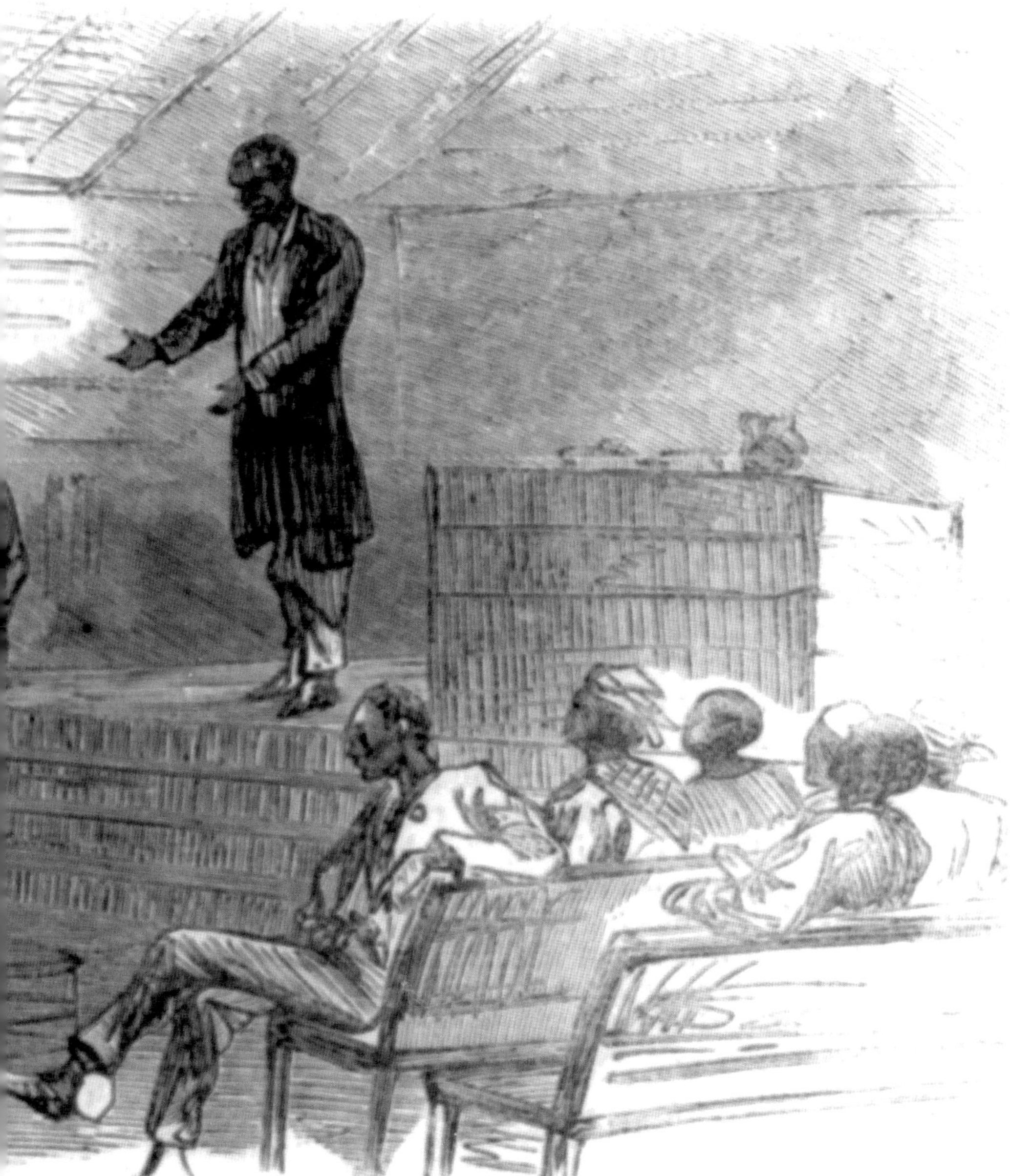

be, the repeal of all laws and parts of laws, State and National that make distinctions on account of color."[136]

Whether he sensed a sudden change in the winds and set his sails accordingly, Holden once again would demonstrate his habit of inconsistency. Two months after he admonished the freedmen to stay out of politics, in the wake of Worth's reelection, Holden and friends, including the rejected senator John Pool, went to see Thaddeus Stevens again. On December 13, Stevens introduced a "North Carolina Enabling Act" that would allow the state back into full Union and put an end to the Worth administration. It called for a "loyal convention" in May to write a new state constitution; whites previously eligible to vote could take part in electing the delegates—and so, if they met a property requirement, could blacks.[137]

That wouldn't be enough.

SCALAWAG AND CARPETBAGGER

As it had in Washington, North Carolina's rejection of the Fourteenth Amendment provoked negative reaction in Greensboro. In his new *Union Register* newspaper, Albion Tourgee denounced the vote and predicted that Congress would deal harshly with North Carolina—a prophecy that he, along with some fellow travelers in the state, tried to help fulfill by petitioning Congress to split the conquered region into new territories in which Union loyalists and former slaves would have the vote while anyone who had held office under the Confederacy would not.

Tourgee had had a busy time since moving south. Soon after settling in Greensboro, he and his wife organized a school for black children that later became Bennett College. Emma read newspapers aloud to the black hands at their nursery. Albion joined a group called the Loyal Reconstruction League, which subsequently affiliated with the national Union League. He railed against the Conservative *Greensboro Patriot* newspaper and, his Ohio roots and newcomer status notwithstanding, got himself elected to a Radical Republican convention for Southern loyalists in Philadelphia.[138]

With Tourgee playing a prominent part, a Guilford County political meeting passed a resolution demanding votes for blacks, and Tourgee spread stories—never substantiated—of freedmen's bodies found in a local pond and of hundreds of Union soldiers who had thought to settle in the state having to flee in fear for their lives.[139] Many Southerners of longer residence found Tourgee a nuisance. John G. Lea of Caswell County described "a bummer named Albion W. Tourgee, of New York, from Sherman's army came to Caswell County and organized a Union League, and they were drilling every night and beating the drums, and he made many speeches telling the negroes that he was sent by the government and that he would see that they got forty acres of land."[140]

A popular Caswell politician, Unionist and former United States senator, Bedford Brown, was part of a delegation that Governor Worth took to Washington in December 1866 to oppose the North Carolina Enabling Act and correct any mistaken impressions left by Holden's visit. Working with several sitting and former Southern governors and congressmen, as well as Andrew Johnson, they came up with a North Carolina Plan alternative to the Fourteenth Amendment. The plan included wording to declare the Union perpetual and required black suffrage, but it also imposed property and educational qualifications on voters that would have effectively left the freedmen outside the polls.[141]

Not only did Congress immediately dismiss the plan, but in March it also passed the Reconstruction Act of 1867—"An Act to Provide for the More Efficient Government of the Rebel States"—which split the South into five military districts, with a general in charge of each, and spelled out how the states were going to Reconstruct themselves. First, each state had to call a constitutional convention of delegates elected by men older than twenty-one years of age who had not been accessory to the Rebel governments—thus including freedmen but leaving out such prominent and experienced men as former governors Vance and Graham. The convention would write a new constitution to Congress's liking, including those rules for voting. The state would ratify the Fourteenth Amendment. Then its representatives could take their places in the United States Capitol.

Johnson vetoed the act. Congress overrode his veto. North Carolina became part of the Second Military District under General Dan Sickles, a veteran who lost a leg at Gettysburg and kept it pickled to show off to guests. Only about fifteen hundred soldiers were dispatched to keep the peace in North Carolina. Sickles made his own headquarters in Charleston, established eleven military posts in North Carolina and in general left Worth to manage the state while imposing some humane measures—he outlawed whipping as criminal punishment and gave debtors extra time to discharge their obligations.

Sickles did accompany the president on a trip to Raleigh, where town elders were dedicating a memorial to Johnson's father, the tavern hostler. Sickles annoyed white citizens by setting up military courts and allowing blacks to serve jury duty in them, but all in all his ruling hand laid so light

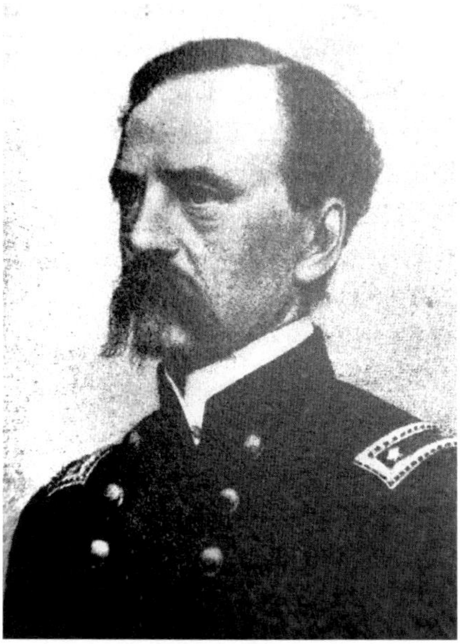

General Dan Sickles, a one-legged Union hero at Gettysburg, got along well with North Carolina officials. *From Hamilton's* History of North Carolina.

on North Carolina that Johnson fired him and sent the more military and less diplomatic General Edwin Canby to take over. The change in command led to little change in practice but did prod the state along by decreeing that the election on whether to hold the constitutional convention, and who would take part in it, would be held in November, ready or not.[142]

North Carolina's new Republican Party was unhappily surprised by how well Sickles and Canby got along with the Worth administration but consoled itself by making ready to take advantage of what Congress had given it. With old Confederates out of electoral politics and new freedmen in, the way to power lay wide open, and Holden had lost no time after his December 1866 Washington trip in endearing himself and his party to the new voters. The *Standard* reported, "It is utterly idle for any citizen of the insurgent States to expect or hope that these States will ever be restored to their former places in the Union until they shall have provided in their fundamental law for absolute equality between the two races as to political and civil rights." On the first day of 1867, he told a meeting of Raleigh freedmen that he was in total support of their right to vote and introduced a resolution calling for the state's new government to be based on "loyal white and black suffrage." Shortly afterward, he promised another black group that their enemies would soon be swept away and their well-being would be in the hands of their friends—for example, Holden.

Oddly enough, no freedmen were formally invited when the Republicans held their first state convention, in March. Responding to black pressure, Holden's newspaper did publish a blanket invitation to blacks and loyal Unionists, and 46 black delegates were on hand to open the convention, along with 101 whites. The *Standard* proclaimed, "Harmony and enthusiasm!! The first step to 'the music of the Union.'" Though some delegates objected to the term "Republican," due to its offensive connotations, Holden overruled them, and the new party so constituted made its platform of congressional

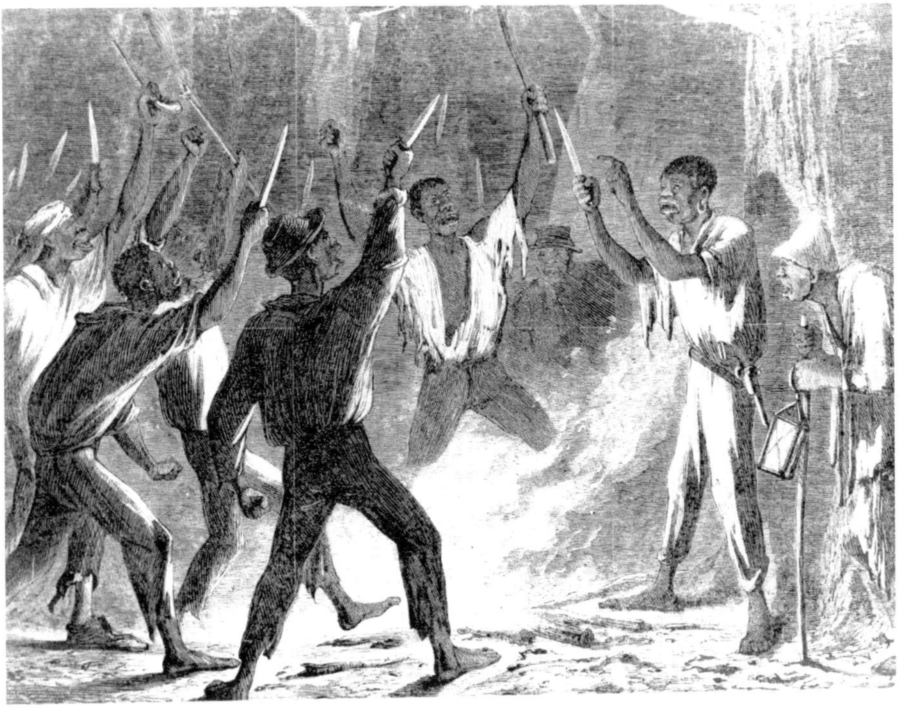

A nighttime meeting of the clandestine Red Strings, an organization of Union sympathizers during the Civil War that was active in Piedmont North Carolina. *Courtesy the North Carolina State Archives.*

Reconstruction and absolute racial equality. Holden, who had already received a federal printing contract, assumed the executive committee chair, overseeing a group of 23 whites and 16 blacks; the *Wilmington Dispatch* described the party as "Holden miscegenationists."[143]

Republican organization brought the Union League into North Carolina's political mainstream. It had a ready base among freedmen and also with the longtime Union sympathizers and the old Heroes of America, or Red Strings, organization. Alamance County was one stronghold for pro-Union sentiment: four days before North Carolina seceded, a group raised a United States flag near the Alamance Battleground, where Royal Governor Tryon had smashed the Regulator insurgents in 1771, and a Greensboro loyalist wrote that the mid-state counties were "unshaken in their devotion to the Stars and Stripes." Some local militiamen took up arms to avoid arrest after refusing to serve for the Confederacy, and a candidate for constable ran on an openly pro-Union platform.

The Heroes of America took their identifying emblem from the Bible story of Rahab, who helped Hebrew spies in Jericho and marked her house with a red cord so she would be spared when the city fell to Joshua and his trumpeting priests. Unionist Red Strings were active in the Alamance-Guilford area soon after the Civil War began, and as homefront conditions deteriorated their presence could become public knowledge with little fear of reprisal. Abraham Clapp won election to the General Assembly in 1864, after a disaffected Red String revealed Clapp's role as an organizer in the group and after Clapp had organized a peace rally that drew more than one thousand people.

The Confederate draft, and Jefferson Davis's suspension of habeas corpus for draft dodgers, gave the dissidents a powerful cause, as they presented themselves as defenders of personal liberty against despots in Richmond and Raleigh. A correspondent to Holden's newspaper, bylining himself "Davie," wrote, "The military go abroad, and without warrant or probable cause, supported by oath, they seize their prisoners, and with all possible speed, convey them to this [prison camp] where the law is dead." Such a populist stance carried on the backcountry tradition, but the Red Strings membership included some men of power and influence, including executives of the North Carolina Railroad and the state saltworks and a general in the state's Home Guard.[144]

There is no documented link between the clandestine Red Strings and the secretive Union League, though there is evidence that whites and blacks cooperated in the Strings' loose wartime network. Wyatt Outlaw, reputedly the mulatto son of Alamance Red String Chesley Faucett, became a Union League leader after the war and leased property for his carpentry shop from another Red String leader, Will Albright. Having set themselves as advocates for the common man and against the Confederacy of plantation interests, former Red Strings would have found some things to like in Holden's new Republicans and their Union League auxiliary, although the Union League served the party most by organizing freedmen into a solid voting bloc and a power base in those areas—such as Caswell County—with large black populations. Holden presided over the Union League's Grand Council for the state and took pains to keep the league aligned with the parent party's interests.

Holden also had pains keeping the party aligned with his own interests. It did not take long for a rift to develop between the Republicans' carpetbagger and scalawag wings. Carpetbaggers like Tourgee, who had come from the North and enjoyed the allegiance of most freedmen, regarded the native scalawags—a term that originally referred to a worthless or maverick horse—

as merely "disfranchised Rebels." Scalawags regarded carpetbaggers—a term originally connoting just a traveling con man—as radical opportunists with no real interest in what was good for the state or its people. Some Republicans of both kinds resented Holden's power and considered him and his protean political history to be a party liability. After Holden took a radical stand at a party convention, coming out in favor of confiscating former Rebel leaders' property if North Carolina did not go along with congressional Reconstruction, some of his scalawag supporters backed off. John Pool and several other moderates and conservatives in the party even published a "Republican Address to the People of North Carolina" to distance themselves from radical elements; Holden, concerned, tried to dismiss the confiscation idea from the state party and attach that onus to Congress.[145]

Worth and his Conservatives enjoyed the spectacle. The *Greensboro Patriot* commented that some of the Republicans "were honest, genuine men, who were bamboozled into the affair to give it *éclat*. The remainder were shams, perfect political mushrooms." The *Raleigh Sentinel*, a newspaper founded in 1865 to "fight against the carpetbaggers," dismissed the Republicans as "old party hacks, broken down, spavined demagogues, mere seekers of office."[146]

But the Conservatives, née Democrats, had schisms of their own. Some leaders, including Worth, sought to curry favor with blacks who would be voting and so divide the Republican bloc. It was a halfhearted attempt, opposed by most of the party, and it accomplished nothing. Conservatives also split over the constitutional convention—Graham, detecting signs of a Democratic comeback in the North, called on white voters to go to the polls and vote against holding a convention, thinking that better terms might be achieved with a different Congress after the 1868 elections. Worth, however, wanted Conservatives to just stay home and have nothing to do with a humiliating process that could only lead to universal black suffrage.[147]

A lot of them did just that, and with Holden laboring for Republican unity—appealing to poor and middle-class whites as well as blacks and driving the party faithful to get out the vote—the convention passed 93,006 to 32,961; of the state's 179,653 registered voters, 53,686 opted out. Orange was one of only two counties where a majority opposed the convention, and Republicans won 107 of the 120 seats there; 15 seats went to African Americans, and even the unreconstructed twentieth-century historian J.G. DeRoulhac Hamilton admitted that some of the black delegates were, "comparatively speaking, men of considerable ability." Of the few Conservatives winning seats, none were prominent political figures; 2 former Confederate soldiers—John W. Graham of Orange County, William Alexander Graham's son; and Plato

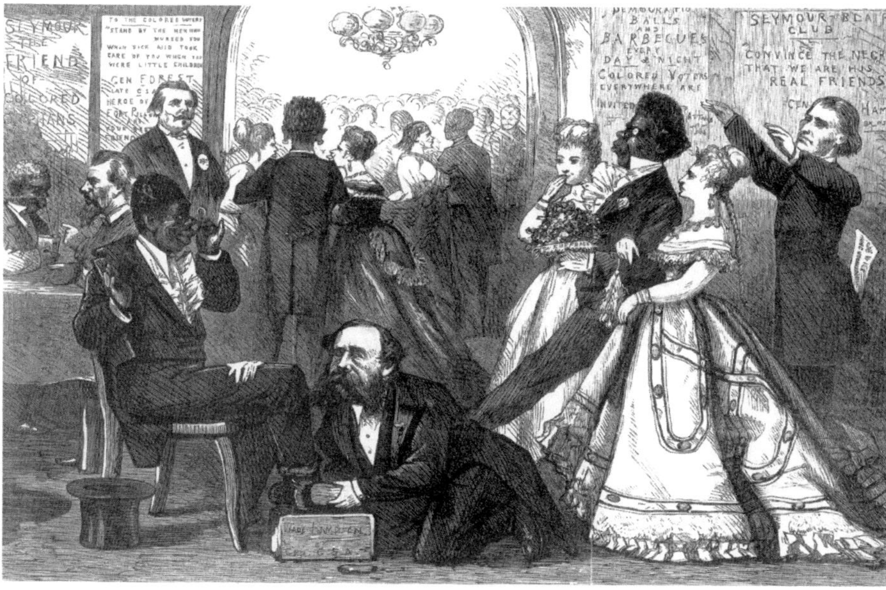

A pair of *Harper's Weekly* cartoons contrasts conflicting Conservative/Democratic attitudes toward the African American vote. *Courtesy the North Carolina State Archives.*

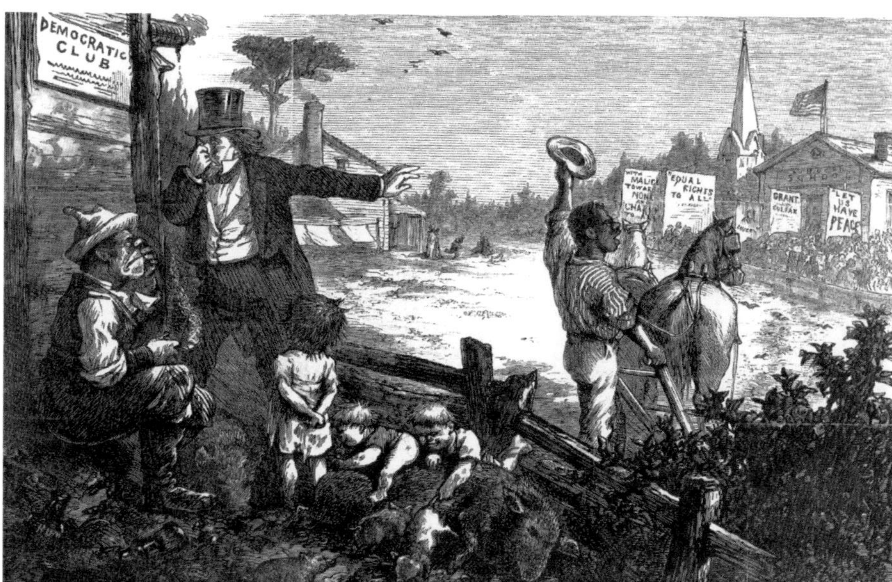

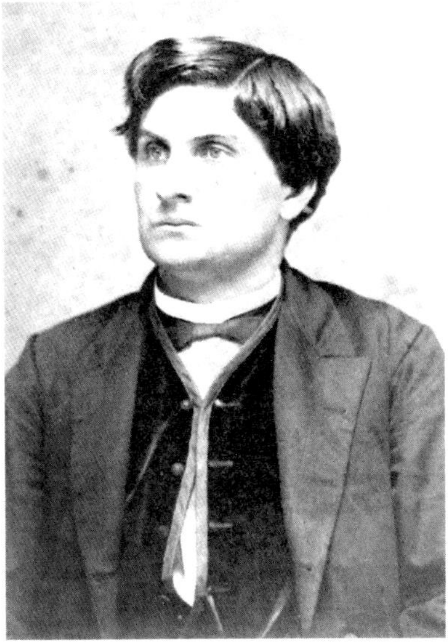

Plato Durham, Conservative from Cleveland County, emerged as a party leader during the state constitutional convention in 1868. *Courtesy the North Carolina State Archives.*

Durham of Rutherford County, at the edge of the mountains—emerged as spokesmen for their side and went on to later prominence in the state.[148] On election day, the *Sentinel* abandoned its neutrality on the race issue and came out in favor of an avowedly white political party. Surprised by the demonstration of Republican strength and organization, Conservatives and other white citizens envisioned an imminent future of property confiscation, civil liberty lost and enforced social equality between whites and blacks.

Tourgee's election as a convention delegate could only have encouraged such misgivings. While winning friends and influencing people in the North and among the freedmen and scalawags, he had alienated his two business associates. Seneca Kuhn and Reuben Pettengill forced Tourgee to buy out their shares in the nursery, which Tourgee had to close shortly thereafter, owing thousands of dollars. Tourgee plowed ahead with his mission, nevertheless, and became one of the new constitution's chief authors after the delegates convened in Raleigh early in 1868—modeling much of the document on that of his native state, Ohio.[149]

By any standard, the new constitution was a liberal one. It outlawed slavery, mandated universal male suffrage and did away with property qualifications for elective office. In a gesture to the American Revolution, it also changed the "House of Commons" to "House of Representatives." The constitution provided that state and county officials were to be elected, eliminating the patronage that had filled many government jobs, and extended the governor's term from two years to four. The convention created a public welfare authority, orphanages and institutions for the care of "all deaf mutes, the blind and the insane." Debtors could no longer be imprisoned; women's property rights were strengthened. Innovations included a public school system requiring at least a four-month annual term; incorporated the state university into the school system; and ordered the addition of agriculture, mechanical, mining and teaching curricula to the higher-education program. Dueling was made a disqualification for public office.[150] Election days would be April 21–23, on ratification and new state officials, using a new voter registration list and putting ratification and elective offices on the same ballot at General Canby's order—an arrangement that led some Conservatives to argue the legality of the whole election as well as the new constitution itself.[151]

While the convention was at work, the *Sentinel* dubbed it "The Convention (So Called)," an epithet that stuck, and said, "The pillars of the Capitol should be hung in mourning today for the murdered sovereignty of North Carolina." When the convention adjourned, the *Sentinel* headlined its coverage:

> *The Disgraceful Closing Scenes!*
> *Corn Field Dance and Ethiopian Minstrelsy!!*
> *Ham Radicalism in its Glory!!!*[152]

The Radicals' opponents organized as the Conservative Union Party. They nominated Samuel Ashe—who had made Holden's acquaintance decades earlier over muffins in Hillsborough—for governor after four other suggested candidates turned them down and made Holden himself—or, rather, his unfitness for office—one of their platform planks, along with defeat of the new constitution and white supremacy. At their organizing convention, the Conservatives proclaimed "negro suffrage and negro equality, if not supremacy," to be "the great and overriding issue" before the people.[153]

The 1868 campaigns were nasty. Holden invoked the disastrous war in painting Conservatives as "desperate" conspirators and war criminals out to extinguish "every noble sentiment of freedom in the colored race." He declared that the Conservatives were reviving "evil passions" of race division that, he claimed by some inattention to detail or rhetorical license, congressional Reconstruction had "so nearly extinguished."

For their part, Conservatives called "White Men, Organize…be true to your Race" and asked, "Shall Negroes or White Men Rule North Carolina?"; "Shall white children be compelled to go to the same schools with negroes?"; "Shall marriage between negroes and whites—amalgamation—be allowed?" The Greensboro *Times* newspaper reported, "If it be treason to hate Holden and the other negro worshippers, then there will be room for a big hanging after the election is over. Holden has deceived every party he ever belonged to, and his putrid carcus [*sic*] was so politically corrupt that even the negroes love him." Tradition says that even the murderer Tom Dula—aka "Tom Dooley" of popular music fame—had told the crowd attending his hanging that Holden's election would bring more ruin upon the state.

Conservatives, according to Tourgee, intimidated blacks and Radicals by "murder, castration, rape, beating and arson."[154] Other historians describe the election as not so physically violent, though Republicans and Conservatives did get into a fistfight after Holden returned to Raleigh from a campaign trip and found himself hanged in effigy. But the campaign did bring out a new element in the state's politics. In majority-black Warren County, open graves began to appear overnight along roads leading to the county seat. In Raleigh and Wilmington, posters appeared:

> *K.K.K.*
> *Attention! First Hour! In the Mist!*
> *At the Flash! Come. Come. Come!*
> *Retribution is impatient! The grave yawns!*
> *The scepter bones rattle!*
> *Let the doomed quake!*[155]

The Ku Klux Klan, formed as a social club in Tennessee in the spring of 1866, soon took on a vigilante role as defenders of the South's old order. Its masked night riding and robed regalia spread to surrounding states, especially after Confederate hero General Nathan Bedford Forrest became the Klan's acknowledged leader, and the group won white sympathy as a counterpoint to the Union League. By some accounts, a North Carolina Ku Klux first formed in Orange County, with one William L. Saunders of Chapel Hill as its leader.[156] It may have formed more or less spontaneously in several places after the constitutional convention. Before the April election, the Lincolnton attorney David Schenck recorded:

> *"Ku Klux Klan" is now organizing through the whole South. Its movements and design are still so mysterious that no one has* [any] *idea of its designs; but by cabalistic signs, methods and advertisements they strike terror into the hearts of the blacks, threatening all manner of punishment even to assassination. They dress in white, move exclusively by night, carry skulls and skeletons around* [and] *use every means to give themselves unnatural character.*[157]

Whatever its theatrics and whatever Tourgee's allegations, the Klan and the Conservatives' white-supremacy campaign went for little. The state's voter roll showed a total registration of 196,872: 117,428 whites and 79,444 blacks. Of these, 85 percent cast ballots. The new constitution won ratification, 93,084 to 74,015. Holden finally got his wish, winning the governorship 92,235 to 73,594—55 percent to 45 percent of the votes cast, and 47 percent of the total electorate. In his inaugural address, he said:

> *Fellow citizens, let us come out of the caverns of the past, and forgetting what is not worthy to be remembered, let us resolve to do our duty in our day and time, as North Carolinians, as Americans. In a climate and with a soil for which providence has done so much, let us resolve to do something for ourselves and our children. Let us devote ourselves to the arts of peace…Let us at least unite upon the one great object of improving and building up the State. Let us welcome capital and immigration, furnishing as they will the indispensable means to our progress and prosperity. Prejudices growing out of nativity, or out of the rebellion, are not worthy to be cherished. Let us discard such prejudices. We are once more Americans—all. Let us receive with courtesy and kindness every citizen of the Northern or Eastern States who may cast his lot among us, and measure him as we measure others, according to his personal and moral worth.*[158]

Republicans carried fifty-eight counties and took control in the legislature by better than three seats to one in the Senate and by two to one in the House. Tourgee had hoped to get a seat in Congress, but state Republican leaders considered him too much of a maverick to toe the party line and set him up instead for a six-year term on a superior court bench, which provided better financial security than a two-year stint in Washington, anyway. It also put Tourgee on point to fight the Ku Klux as it made itself busier and bloodier in 1869 and 1870.[159]

Some credit for the Republican success was due John Walter Stephens, an indefatigable Republican and Union League worker in the trenches of Caswell County who had come under Tourgee's sway. The circumstances of their meeting are not known; perhaps Stephens, though a lifelong Southerner, had been moved by one of Tourgee's passionate speeches. In any case, the two men met along some campaign trail and struck up, if not a friendship, at least a relationship of mentor (Tourgee) and mentee (Stephens). Stephens was barely literate, but the carpetbagging attorney tutored Stephens in the basics of the law, gave him a bar exam and, having become Judge Tourgee, made Stephens a justice of the peace. According to the defamatory Stephens biography by Greensboro *Patriot* editor Andrew Stedman, Stephens paid Tourgee twenty dollars for his law license; according to the laudatory Tourgee biography by Wagner College historian Mark Elliott, the two men boarded together.

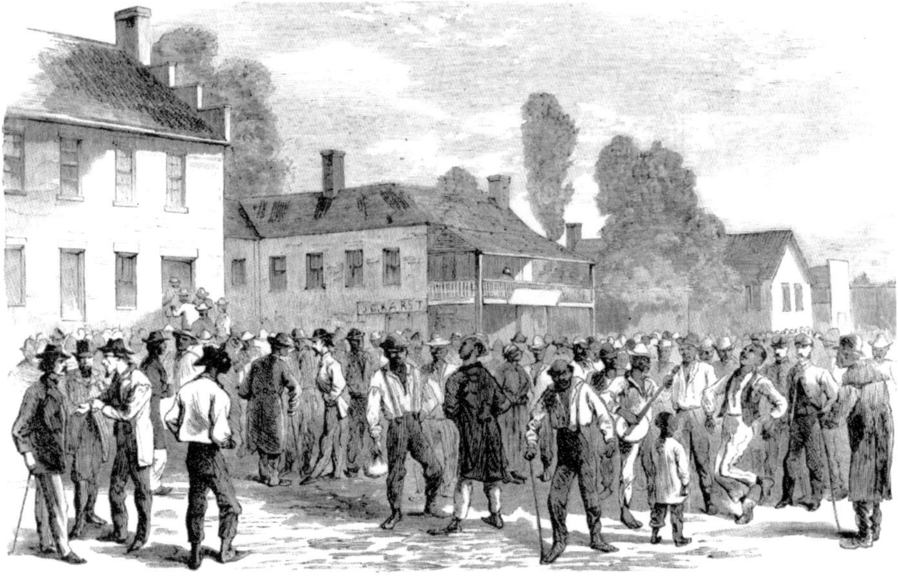

Black men register to vote in Asheville, 1867. The Union League organized freedmen into a political bloc to back the Republican Party. *Courtesy the North Carolina State Archives.*

The association did nothing to improve Tourgee's standing among his neighbors. The rest of the state bar "considered it beneath the dignity of so high an official to make his home with a man so low on the social scale… They insisted that they would have treated him with respect, if not with cordiality, had he not shown these degraded tastes."[160]

Stephens's sympathetic biographer, Luther M. Carlton, skips this part of Stephens's career, while Stedman reports that, as a magistrate, Stephens was "austere, repressive and arbitrary" and, as a person, "unpleasant, unpopular, disagreeable and odious." He would make himself considerably more so.

Accounts of Stephens's life are sketchy and highly colored by their authors' opinions but are in agreement on the basic facts. He was born near Bruce's Crossroads, a hamlet in northern Guilford County, on October 14, 1834. His parents were Absalom and Letitia Stephens, and John was one of six children—four sons and two daughters—born to the couple. Absalom was a tailor by trade, and the family moved about: to Wentworth, in Rockingham County to the north, and then to Leaksville, near the Virginia line, where Absalom died in 1848, leaving "the invaluable legacy of a good name."[161]

Absalom had been a Mason, and upon his death the lodge gave the family a house in Leaksville. John received an education "of a very ordinary sort" but studied on his own, and as an adult he said he had "often mourned his lack of education" and described his lack as "what every poor man owed to slavery."[162] He stood five feet, ten inches tall, weighed 140 pounds and had a fair complexion, blue eyes, light hair and, as a young man, "an amiable disposition, but, when aroused, he became daring and reckless."[163]

Moving back to Wentworth, Stephens went into the harness- and shoe-making business and, in 1857, married Nannie (or Nancy) Walters, who died two years later after bearing a daughter. He married again, in 1860, this time to Frances Groom, formerly of Caswell County, who gave him a second daughter. Raised a Methodist, he was active in the church and worked for a year as an agent for the American Bible and Tract Society in Rockingham and Caswell Counties before becoming a tobacco trader and moving the family to South Carolina.[164]

By this time, Stephens had demonstrated a cagey head for business—by one account, he swindled "a good Quaker gentleman" named T.J. Benbow out of seventy-five dollars' worth of leather. By another account, though, "He was known by all as an honest, fair-dealing, Christian man…a most loving husband and kind father." Stephens moved back to North Carolina when the Civil War began and went to work for the Confederate army as a "press agent"—not in the present-day sense of publicity but in the 1861 sense of "impressing," or commandeering, horses and mules for military use, having paid a substitute to take his place in uniform.

Stephens had a neighbor named Thomas Ratliff, and toward Stephens there may have been some bad feeling on the part of Ratliff's brother William, who had lost out to Stephens for the press agent job. An interfamily grudge may have aggravated a dispute between the neighbors over chickens. Thomas Ratliff owned a large flock of the birds, which regularly crossed the property line to feed in Stephens's barn and raid his garden. Stephens complained, Ratliff did nothing and, upon finding his barn full of Ratliff poultry one morning, Stephens killed two and offered them to Ratliff's wife.

Mrs. Ratliff had a conniption fit and refused Stephens's offer, whereupon Stephens took the dead chickens to his own house and had them plucked, dressed and cooked. Meanwhile, Mr. Ratliff learned of the deed, went to the courthouse and swore out a warrant for Stephens's arrest as a chicken thief. The local constabulary did its duty; Stephens spent the night in jail and posted a $500 bond the following morning.

Going home, Stephens saw Ratliff outside his store, picked up a pistol and a heavy walking stick, went back to Ratliff's place of business and whacked

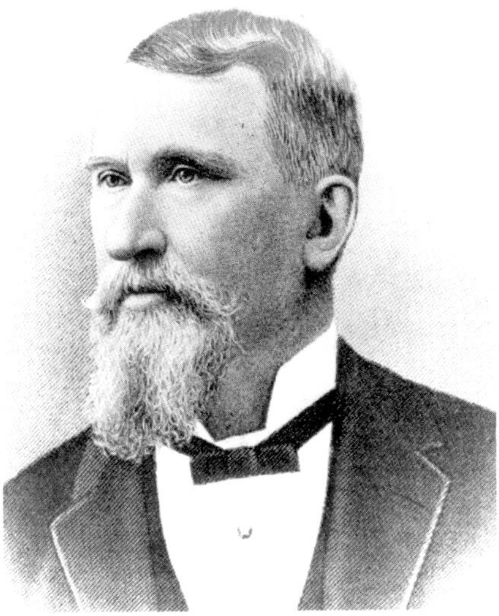

For decades, this image has been identified as John Walter "Chicken" Stephens, but according to the Caswell Historical Association it's not him after all. *Courtesy the North Carolina State Archives.*

him on the head. A bystander saw the assault and got himself between the men. Stephens started shooting and hit both the would-be peacemaker and a boy passing by. Neither wound was serious, but Stephens was back in the hands of the law. This time he spent two nights in jail and posted a $2,000 bond. It was now February 1865, the war was going badly and Stephens was caught in the Confederate draft. He spent an uneventful hitch in service and went back to trading tobacco in Wentworth. Apparently, he was never summoned to court for the fowl incident, but he did come out of it with the nickname "Chicken," which stuck with him ever since.

In 1866, perhaps to escape the Guilford County authorities, Stephens moved the family and one of his sisters to Caswell County. They settled in Yanceyville, but the sister soon returned to Wentworth. A former Wentworth neighbor claimed that the sister had been mistreated under Stephens's roof. However, his mother did move in with them, Stephens having persuaded her to sell the house the Masonic lodge had given her and give him the proceeds in return for perpetual care. Letitia suffered from debilitating spasms.

It was just about this time that Stephens became a Republican convert. He also joined the Union League and became an agent of the Freedmen's Bureau, thus associating closely with blacks, scalawags and carpetbaggers such as Albion Tourgee. His Yanceyville neighbors and co-religionists began to talk, in the small-town way, and soon Stephens found himself held in general contempt. Townsman Allen Gunn, a Methodist and a Conservative, attempted to convince the errant sinner to change his ways; Stephens said that he was only in it for the money, that the Conservatives were behind the times and, by the way, that for $4,000 he would ensure a Conservative win in the next election.

The church kicked him out.[165]

CORRUPTION AND KU KLUX

William Woods Holden had been a party boss, polemicist and power broker. Now, in April 1868, his ambition was rewarded with what he had sought so long—governorship by popular will, notwithstanding the fact that enough voters to have turned the count against him had sat the election out.

Even some of the opposition press was ready to give him the benefit of the doubt. Aside from blacks and Republicans, Holden's campaign attracted a sizable bloc of white voters—maybe as many as thirty-five thousand—ready to put the war, secession and politics behind, restore North Carolina to its place in the United States and have peace and quiet for a change. With the election done, the Conservative *Western Democrat* of Charlotte opined, "The great mass of the people want quiet and rest," and warned that partisan opposition to the duly elected governor would only perpetuate civil and social conflict.

That, though, was a minority report. In Raleigh, the lame-duck governor Worth spoke of "dregs of society" coming to power and predicted anarchy to come. In Greensboro, David Frank Caldwell, an old Unionist, wrote that freedom was lost and that it must have been divine wrath that allowed "such an unblushing creature as W.W. Holden" to occupy the state's highest office. Benjamin Hedrick had been a state university professor until his prewar antislavery sentiments led Holden to denounce him as "impudent and highly objectionable" and recommend his termination; now, in 1868, Hedrick reminded Congress that Holden had in the past supported slavery

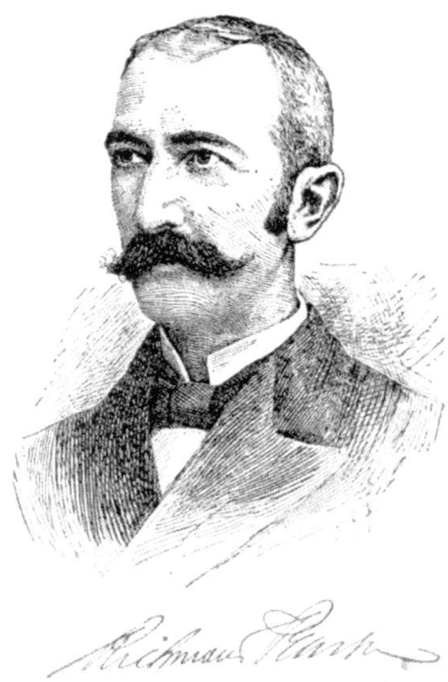

North Carolina chief justice Richmond Pearson was a friend of Holden but upheld the rule of habeas corpus against him. *Courtesy the North Carolina State Archives.*

and states' rights and even claimed that, as provisional governor, he had done all he could to restore Rebel Democrats to power.

Congressional Republicans paid scant attention. They praised Holden for recognizing and repenting the error of his ways and approved North Carolina's new constitution. Holden, in Washington to solidify his support there, joined in the Radical hue and cry for impeaching Andrew Johnson—the president Holden had praised in 1865 as "a man of first-rate ability, possessed of an iron will, and enthusiastically devoted, as his whole public life shows, to the rights and interests of the people." Even before the state constitution passed Congress, Holden had called for the legislature to meet on July 1 to ratify the Fourteenth Amendment, the next step toward regaining statehood. In late June, General Canby directed the state's newly elected chief justice, Richmond M. Pearson, to take up his office and swear Holden in.

Worth, who with other Conservatives detested the "Canby constitution," had considered refusing to turn the state over to Holden, "with the view of raising the question as to the constitutionality of the law under which he claims to be elected." Not trusting the state's courts in the event of his arrest, Worth decided to go, but not without protest when Holden, having just delivered his inaugural address, arrived to pick up the office keys.[166]

Worth gave Holden a letter and asked that it be recorded in the governor's official papers. It quoted a telegram that Worth had received from Canby on June 30, ordering that Holden become governor on July 1. Worth told Holden that he surrendered the office only under "military duress." The letter read in part:

> *I do not recognize the validity of the last election, under which you and those co-operating with you claim to be invested with the civil government of the State. You have no evidence of your election save the certificate of a Major*

> *General of the United States army. I regard all of you as, in effect, appointees of the military of the United States, and not as "deriving your powers from the consent of those you claim to govern." Knowing, however, that you are backed up by military force here, which I could not resist if I would, I do not deem it necessary to offer a futile opposition, but vacate the office without the ceremony of actual eviction, offering no further opposition than this, my protest. I would submit to actual expulsion in order to bring before the Supreme Court of the United States the question as to the constitutionality of the legislation under which you claim to be the rightful governor of the State, if the past action of that tribunal furnished any hope of a speedy trial. I surrender the office to you under what I deem military duress, without stopping, as the occasion would justify, to comment upon the singular coincidence that the present State Government is surrendered as without legality to him whose own official sanction, but three years ago, declared it valid.*[167]

Grudgingly or not, Worth gave the keys to Holden and left. The exultant Republicans mixed a victory rally with Independence Day celebration, and the new governor praised the Union, preserved on a basis of liberty for all Americans "of whatever origin, color or former condition." He warned of another civil war if anyone tried to take the freedmen's newly won rights away but remarked that harmony would prevail "if everyone will faithfully submit to the Constitution and the laws." He claimed that whites would lose their fear of and opposition to black suffrage once they realized it was no bad thing after all.

Taking command, Holden undertook to implement some of the progressive innovations he had advocated and encouraged the legislature to take the lead on others: the insane asylum, a state penitentiary, protections for labor from exploitive employers, public schools and encouraging Northern capital and manpower into the state. His success rate was spotty, hampered by legislative lethargy, the state's pinched finances and, in some cases, public opinion.[168]

A case in point is Holden's attempt to revive the university in Chapel Hill, whose academic gentry were still scandalized over the marriage of President David Swain's daughter, Eleanor, to General Smith B. Atkins, commander of the Union occupation troops. In 1865, with troopers in blue stabling horses in the university library and grazing them on the campus lawn, Atkins went to pay a courtesy call on Swain and was instantly smitten with Ellie, and she with him. As recorded by Cornelia Phillips Spencer, they spent the summer courting, and each evening the army band played a serenade outside her window. Atkins wrote her:

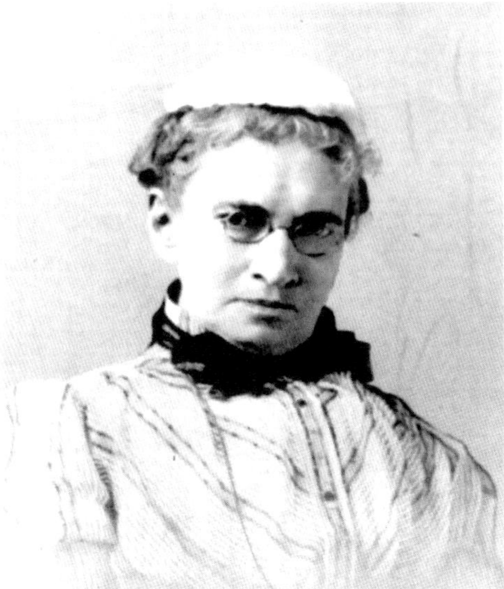

Cornelia Phillips Spencer of Chapel Hill wrote of the Civil War and a scandalous romance that followed. *Courtesy the North Carolina State Archives.*

> *The best artillery is found*
> *to be the oldest,*
> *And Peace hath conquests*
> *too, by no means narrow,*
> *The wisest soldier, &*
> *perchance the boldest,*
> *Yields to a pair of blue eyes,*
> *and a bow & arrow.*[169]

Tongues wagged all over town, especially when the bewildered father, not knowing how to handle this situation, showed some of the couple's correspondence around town. Ellie was aghast at the indiscretion, and when invitations went out for the Swain-Atkins wedding in August, some recipients spat upon them. The handful of students on hand rang the school bell all through the wedding service and afterward hanged Swain and Atkins in effigy. The couple moved to Illinois.

> *The blight that immediately fell upon the university was directly attributable to the fact that* [Swain] *not only permitted his daughter to marry an invader, but that he gave her a fine wedding. It was told from mouth to mouth and believed all over North Carolina that Ellie Swain went to Illinois loaded with finery and jewels stolen from the women of states further south, and given to her by her husband.*[170]

Far in debt and with only about one hundred students—a quarter of its antebellum enrollment—the university was also, in Holden's eyes, still under control of Rebel elements, the same people who had driven Professor Hedrick from his classroom. Perhaps Holden had forgotten his own part in that decision; in any case, he appointed a new board of trustees sympathetic to Republican interests, and the new board promptly fired Swain and closed the school until its administration could be reorganized. After classes resumed in March 1869, a total of thirty-five students enrolled.[171]

By then, Swain had died after his buggy—drawn by a horse given him by W.T. Sherman, to further scandal in Chapel Hill—overturned. Spencer recorded that the town's society disintegrated and more than thirty families had moved away in the first weeks after Swain's death and Holden's reorganization. The few students hardly bothered to study, and professors went unpaid. Solomon Pool, a former mathematics professor and the brother of Holden ally John Pool, became the new president. Considering the diminutive student body, Pool declared that he would admit black students if no whites would come. It was an empty threat, the cautious governor and board having decided to establish a separate black college rather than risk antagonizing white Republicans. When commencement time came in 1870, there was no one to graduate, and the following winter, Holden's revival program a total failure, the university closed down.[172]

With that development more than two years in the future, Holden, freshly in office and having stated his commitment to peace and prosperity, went about firming up his authority and in the process antagonizing many of those he had been elected to govern. He sold his newspaper for $15,000 to a Republican group led by Milton S. Littlefield, a former Union general who had come south in search of opportunity and operated a bar in one of the Capitol building's committee rooms.[173]

He revoked Worth's appointments of the state's directors on railroad boards and replaced them with his own friends—though private stockholders in the Western North Carolina blocked Holden's appointment of his son-in-law, Calvin Cowles, to be company president. The governor groused about "rebel stockholders." Holden also kicked Worth allies out of county and municipal positions and installed Republicans until elections could be held. He was upheld in his patronage by the friendly legislature. Looking ahead to the fall elections, he said that he was concerned about violence at the polls and asked the General Assembly's permission to organize a militia and county police squads.

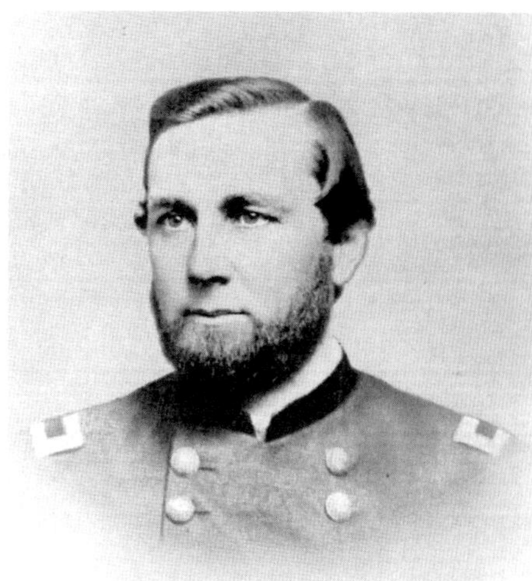

Milton S. Littlefield, "Prince of Carpetbaggers," connived with George Swepson to take control of North Carolina's legislature and railroads. *Courtesy the North Carolina State Archives.*

Even some Holden supporters were put off by the governor's "mischief" based on "his own fears and a heart bent on vindictiveness" and by the threat to the same civil liberties Holden had defended so fiercely against the Confederate government a few years earlier. Conservatives, too, called Holden on his affront to rights and liberties and charged that he was calculating "to invoke the country in a disastrous civil war." The legislators agreed to the governor's militia but drew the line at local police.[174]

Conservatives were also looking ahead to fall's election season. Johnson had survived impeachment still in office but had no chance of any party's nomination. Never-say-die Southerners hoped for a Democratic victory in November that would put the Radicals out of power and replace them with a new Congress that would undo some of their Reconstruction work. North Carolina Conservatives, shocked out of their sulks by the Republican landslide in April, entered autumn with real hope, invigorated when new Chief Justice Pearson advised them to vote for the Republican, Ulysses S. Grant, to avoid the Civil War's resumption. The federal Reconstruction acts had been unconstitutional, Pearson wrote, but a conquered people had to accept whatever was put upon them.[175]

Grant won a majority of North Carolina's popular vote, but his opponent, Democrat Horatio Seymour, won about eleven thousand votes more than Ashe had in his loss to Holden for governor—evidence of the Conservatives' revival as a political force. The state's Republicans did not give any sign of being troubled, though. Holden went so far at a victory party in Raleigh as to almost bait the Klan: "Nobody is afraid of them now. The truth is, we never were afraid of them."

Perhaps not, but in mid-October Holden issued a proclamation:

> *Information has been received at this department that military weapons, such as repeating rifles of various kinds, have been imported into this State, and have been distributed with ammunition and equipments to citizens in several localities. It is believed that boxes containing arms, ammunition and equipments are concealed in divers places, ready to be distributed as opportunity may offer.*
>
> *The object of the persons thus engaged must be either to subvert the government, to resist the constituted authorities, or to prevent a free election in this State on the third day of next month…*
>
> *When, in time of peace, weapons of an extraordinary character are imported into the State by political organizations, and deposited and distributed in a secret manner among persons whose spokesmen deny the*

> *authority of the existing government, and who publicly declare that all government, to be authoritative and binding, must proceed alone from one race of our people, a state of affairs is at once constituted which renders it the duty of every officer and every citizen to be more than usually vigilant…*
>
> *If it be the purpose of any portion of the people, by the use of arms, or by threats, or intimidation, to prevent the people from going to the polls and voting as they may choose to vote on the third day of next month, it is my duty to inform them that force will be met with force, and that every person who may thus violate the law will be punished.*[176]

Holden had ordered arms himself, with which to equip his militia. But election day had been peaceable, and some tension went out of the state while some had been tightened. In December, Holden's antagonist Josiah Turner bought the *Raleigh Sentinel* to continue its attacks on Republicans and Reconstruction. In Caswell County, the grand old Bedford Brown had run for state senate against the county's number-one Republican, Chicken Stephens. Brown, who had suspended his political career when North Carolina seceded, won; but Republicans accused him of election fraud, and when he went to Raleigh the legislature refused to seat him and took Stephens in his place. That was the point at which Stephens, after receiving his first death threats, fortified his house. He wrote Holden:

> *I wish to call your particular attention to the condition I have placed myself in by cuming* [sic] *out & standing up for the Republican party in this Co. & ask your support & protection in the matter. before I taken this stand (whitch I did because I thought it was rite & have never yet regretted and hope I never shall) I had money friends & credit for anything I wanted but now I have neither the trouth is that I have not means to buy what I actuly kneed for the support of my family. my creditors have pushed on me and taken everything that the law would allow & I can look to know source but the Republican party if theire is any thin you can do for me in this hour of kneed pleas let me know what it is.*[177]

Holden made Stephens part of a detective team he engaged to keep tabs on Ku Klux activity, a service for which Stephens reputedly made seven dollars a day.[178] Stephens also arrived at the legislature in time to pick up some of the cash that was flowing around to ease the way of railroad bonds promoted by Littlefield as an agent for speculator George W. Swepson and others involved in what came to be known as the Ring.

Holden had promised North Carolina many things—schools, orphanages, internal improvements—but by the time he took office the state was $14.9 million in debt. Nevertheless, in 1868 the state put its good name and what credit rating it had behind bonds of the incomplete Wilmington, Charlotte and Rutherford line along the state's southern edge. It lent the Northwestern North Carolina Railroad, to run west from Greensboro toward the Appalachian escarpment, $50,000 for every five miles of track it laid as far as Salem, about thirty miles away. Immediate aid to other railroads added almost $2 million to the state's obligations, plus it had donated its interest in the Cape Fear and Deep River Navigation Company to the Chatham Railroad Company in the state's midsection.[179]

The legislature's generosity was encouraged by more than $240,000 that Swepson and Littlefield spread among its members. Littlefield got a commission on every bond approved, reward for lobbying services that he and founding state Republican Byron Laflin performed in the interest of Swepson's maneuvering. In the project, Swepson was collaborating with railroad executives, lawyers and assorted politicians. He ingratiated himself with Republicans by announcing support for Grant in the presidential race and by putting up most of the purchase cash for Holden's newspaper; on the other hand, he also gave financial aid to Josiah Turner when he sought to buy the rival *Sentinel* and courted and won the favor of Augustus Summerfield Merrimon, chairman of the Conservative Union Party's executive committee.[180]

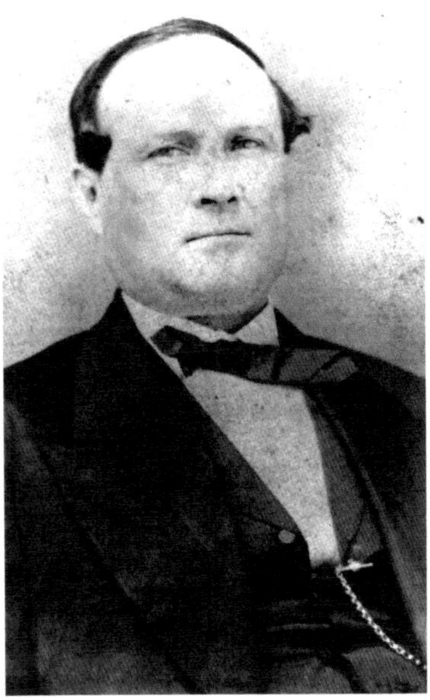

State legislator Augustus Summerfield Merrimon fell for the railroad-bond scam and later helped prosecute William Holden. *Courtesy the North Carolina State Archives.*

Swepson was a Virginian by birth, but by the age of twenty-one he was farming in Caswell County and owned $9,000 worth of real estate. In Caswell, he married Virginia Bartlett Yancey, daughter of the county seat's namesake, Bartlett Yancey, one of the state's most prominent public figures of the 1820s and '30s. Twenty years later, according to the 1860 federal census, the Swepsons were living in Alamance County and owned about $70,000 worth of land and personal property. Dabbling in banking and other speculations, he

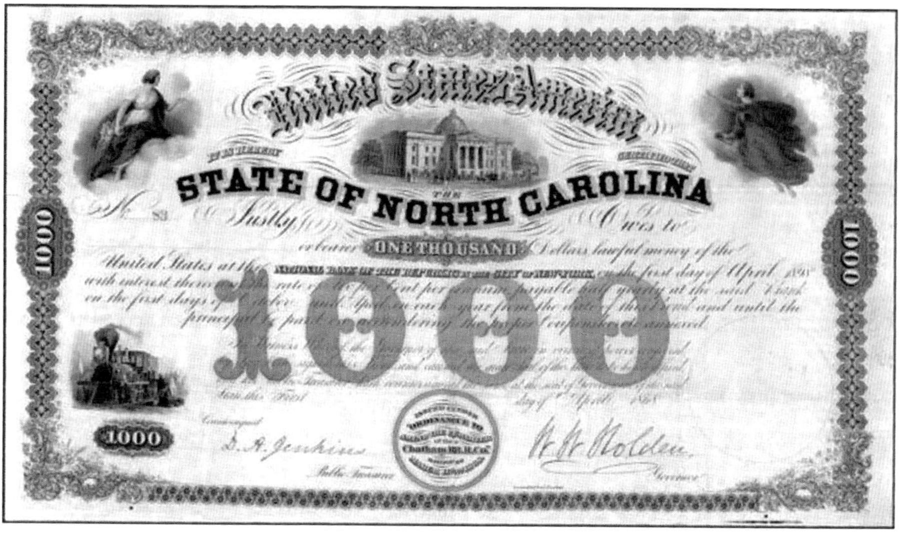

A North Carolina railroad bond, issued over William Holden's signature. The state lost millions when the bond market collapsed. *Courtesy Caswell County Historical Association.*

developed a large circle of business people and influential citizens who served him well when he appeared in Raleigh in 1868.[181]

Swepson dazzled Holden, Merrimon and others with a vision of a Southern railroad network connecting North Carolina's two small ports with the Mississippi River. Rather than building railroads with the state's money, though, Swepson's Ring bought stock in more railroads, speculated in the bond market, awarded construction contracts for which no work was ever done, or expected, and all in all enjoyed the ill-gotten wealth—running much of it through banks that Swepson controlled. Their idea was to bankrupt the railroads in which the state's taxpayers were invested, to the eventual tune of $27.8 million, and then buy them up at a fraction of their value.

Holden caught on to none of this; though he was concerned as the state's debt rose and rose, he felt sure that a new property tax would protect North Carolina's solvency. He told the legislators that an assessment underway would show real estate worth $250 million that would put $1 million a year into the public coffers. Imagine his dismay when the assessment totaled only $79,557,344, produced less than half the revenue he expected and left the government to find more than $500,000 to cover interest on the state debt. The legislature didn't bother to cooperate, and the state defaulted on its payments, damaging its credit standing and sending its railroad bonds into a collapse that only ended with them going for 2.8 percent of par.[182]

Even North Carolina legislators were irate, first demanding an investigation of Holden's state treasurer, David A. Jenkins. Jenkins was cleared of wrongdoing, after Littlefield hustled a key witness out of town, but it was revealed that William Robbins, who started the probe, had taken money from Chicken Stephens for help with campaign expenses. His muckraking sensibilities alerted, Josiah Turner set his *Sentinel* on the Capitol's rascals, calling for the expulsion of another probe proponent, the carpetbagger William Sweet, for damaging the state senate's reputation. But by the fall of 1869, John W. Graham—William Alexander's son, who had come to notice during the constitutional convention—and other legislators were demanding a full investigation of the railroad scandal.[183]

Holden, ignoring or oblivious of the fact that he was, again, feeding ammunition to his enemies, tried to block any such proceeding. He had convinced himself that politics, and attempts to discredit his administration, were the sole motivation for Graham and other Conservatives, even though some Republicans were calling for the facts to be brought out and any culprits brought to justice. Holden's influence was enough to practically neuter the fact-finding committees that the General Assembly finally did appoint, and they found no evidence of fraud that would stand up in court. Nevertheless, in the public mind, Holden, the Republicans and everything they stood for bore stigma for graft and corruption.[184]

Raiders of the people's treasury were one source of trouble for the governor. The white vigilantes were another. Encouraged by the resurgent Conservative Party and friendly local authorities, groups going by the names of White Brotherhood, Constitutional Union Guard and Invisible Empire—called collectively the Ku Klux Klan—were recruiting members and carrying out the occasional show of strength, such as whipping a Union Leaguer in Alamance County who had opened a freedmen's school and tried to integrate the seating at three churches. The offender,

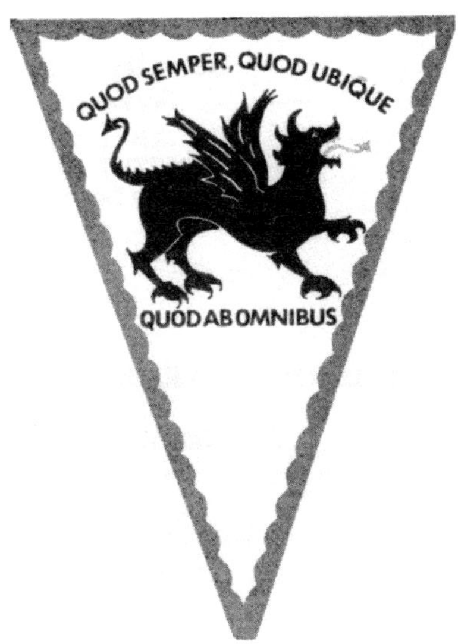

Ku Klux Klan banner of the 1860s. *After an illustration in Zuber's* North Carolina During Reconstruction.

Alonzo Corliss, received a visit in October 1868 and found himself lashed, dragged into the woods and getting his head half-shaved and painted with tar. Subsequently, a flag bearing a picture of a coffin appeared at Corliss's school, with a notice: "Corliss and the Negroes: Let the guilty beware."[185]

The following February, the White Brotherhood held a parade in Graham, the Alamance County seat, during which members brandished firearms and shot at local officials. In response, Republicans, Red Stringers and emerging Union League leader Wyatt Outlaw organized themselves as vigilantes, mounting patrols and enforcing a nighttime curfew. Holden sent militiamen and some of his detectives to help out,[186] and the *Sentinel* accused him of inflicting black rule on the citizens.

Several weeks after the Graham parade, on April 12, the legislature made it a crime to go masked, disguised or painted on the public roads, and Holden made a second address to the citizens on violent vigilantism: "Bands of men who go masked and armed at night, causing alarm and terror in neighborhoods, and committing acts of violence on the inoffensive and defenceless...depredators and robbers, who lived on the honest earnings of others." Such as those, the governor promised, would be "made to feel the penalty due to their crimes." But he also asked for the people's goodwill:

> *Public opinion properly embodied and expressed will be more effectual in repressing these evils, and in promoting the general good...than the execution of the law itself...I call upon every citizen to unite with me in discountenancing disorders and violence of all kinds, and fostering and promoting confidence, peace and good will among the whole people.*[187]

The next month, a carpetbagger sheriff and a black man who happened to be with him were gunned down in an eastern county. Holden sent in the militia, but as soon as it withdrew, another carpetbagger, who had organized a black group in reaction to night riders, died at Ku Klux hands. Northern financiers, reading of returning insurrection and chaos in Dixie, directed their investments—the capital that Holden had invited in his inaugural speech—away from the slowly rebuilding Southern economy and into safer areas like the Wild West. The immigrants Holden sought for skills and muscle went elsewhere.[188] Holden pondered what to do, and with whom. His plans and his people were in danger. And there were elections coming up to think about.

THE KU KLUX EXPERIENCE

And in October, 1869, I deemed it my duty to issue another proclamation, setting forth the fact that in the Counties of Lenoir, Jones, Orange and Chatham, "there is, and has been for some months past, a feeling of insubordination and insurrection, insomuch that many good citizens are put in terror for their lives and property, and it is difficult, if not impossible, to secure a full and fair enforcement of the law." I gave notice in this proclamation that violations of law and outrages in the aforesaid Counties must cease; otherwise I would "proclaim those Counties in a state of insurrection" and would "exert the whole power of the State to enforce the law, to protect those who are assailed or injured, and to bring criminals to justice."[189]

Confronted with proliferating vigilantism that enforced laws—or whims—of its own, the scandal-ridden, debt-laden governor of the mercurial disposition and checkered political past faced several dilemmas. He had to do something. As governor, he was responsible for upholding and enforcing the state's law; unchecked, the criminal violence undermined his authority and credibility as North Carolina's chief executive; his power base of African Americans, carpetbaggers, scalawags and other citizens who just wanted peace and order was scared, with good reason; his career was in jeopardy; and, being a pious Christian, he was certainly just plain outraged.

Moreover, his options were limited. In county after county, enforcers of the law themselves were members of, or at least in cahoots with, a Klan unit of one local name or another. His militia was not large; its loyalty, too,

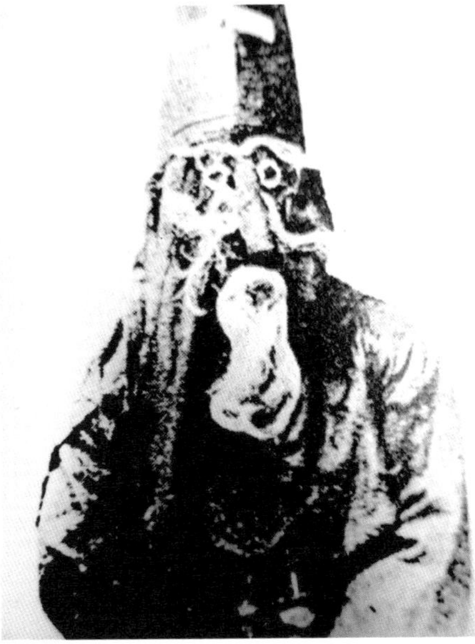

A Ku Kluxer in Reconstruction regalia. Local authorities could not, or chose not to, curb the night riders' terror tactics. *From Hamilton's* History of North Carolina.

was questionable; and Holden had no power to dispatch it until county authorities asked him to do so.

So he complained that Washington and the North in general did not understand how it was in the late Confederacy and that Congress should have sent a larger occupation force. In November 1868, he wrote Secretary of War William W. Belknap: "A regiment of infantry, and four companies of cavalry, stationed at different points, would have a most salutary effect."[190] But the new Grant administration was loath to intervene, and Holden was on his own. He sent out his detectives and issued proclamations from Raleigh.

Those had little effect, if any, out in the state where the Klan was building what would have been, had it been organized and coordinated, a guerilla army. Ku Klux membership was estimated, at its Reconstruction peak in 1869–70, as high as forty thousand.[191] Citizens who had experienced Yankee invasion firsthand, along the route of Sherman's march in the east or that of General George Stoneman in the west; disempowered old Democrats; grudge-bearing Confederate veterans; whites preached at for generations to fear and look down on blacks; upheaval in the fundamental ways of life provoking people to fall back on old habits of thought and seek order in the past—all made fertile ground for an ideology and organization offering revenge and affirmation.

Ku Kluxing spanned the social spectrum, in membership and in victims. The Lincolnton lawyer David Schenck joined up;[192] so did Thaddeus Redmond of Orange County, illegitimate son of a disreputable saloonkeeper.[193] Klan targets included blacks, such as the unfortunate sheriff's companion; whites working on blacks' behalf, such as Corliss; and businesspeople, such as a railroad contractor from Virginia whose tracks were repeatedly attacked by Klan riders.

For Schenck and men like him, the motivation to join may have been politics; for others, such as Redmond, a shoemaker who, as a Confederate sergeant, fell wounded in Pickett's Charge at Gettysburg, night riding might have been a way to relive war's invigoration and break a humdrum routine. Imagining some thrilling days of yesteryear, a reporter telling Redmond's story wrote: "White-robed horsemen with a fiery cross emblazoned on their costumes became familiar figures along lonely stretches of lowland roads and through winding pathways of the more mountainous sections of the country. Sometimes they rode singly, sometimes in two, and not infrequently in groups of 15 and 20."

According to "Major" Redmond and "Senator" James E. Lyon, Reconstruction Kluxers who reminisced for a newspaper story in 1929, Orange County had three Klan groups: the Cain Creek, the Eno and the Durham, organized by the Chapel Hill ex-Confederate William Saunders. Saunders got the nickname "Wild Bill" and rose to become nominal head of the statewide Ku Klux network. Some of their recollections were prankish, such as tossing bottles of beer over the wall to friends in a prison yard; some were personally amusing:

> *One of Major Redmond's favorite stories has to do with a mid-night ride of his on a "gangly colt" which in some details put that of Paul Revere to shame. The Yankees had come through the county and as was their custom had confiscated all of the horses and other livestock that they could carry along on which would add in any manner to their equipage. They left with the Major, however, a colt.*
>
> *One night about sundown, he received a notice to go about 30 miles into Chatham county. There was nothing to ride but the colt, but the major was not to be daunted. He set out. He rode all night and never reached his destination. Fortunately, the Negro uprising which was expected in the Chatham district did not develop. The major says the memory of that night spent on the back of "that gangly colt" will not soon be forgotten.*

Other old memories were not funny at all.

> *Two Negroes, Jeff and Dan Morrow, were suspected of incendiarism in connection with the burning of a barn on the farm of William Jones near Cain creek. They were caught and brought to trial by the klan. Never once, says Senator Lyon, was there in his recollection an instance of punishment being meted out without trial. They were found guilty and hanged, one on*

> *one tree and the other on another tree. The man whose barn had been burned knew nothing of the meeting of the klan and the swiftness with which justice had been meted out. The next morning when he went to his barn lot he noticed the two lifeless forms of two Negroes swinging from the trees.*[194]

James E. Boyd, an Alamance County Kluxer who turned against the group, described his initiation into the White Brotherhood before a U.S. Senate committee:

> *The oath set out by swearing me never to reveal the name of the person who initiated me. It went on by making me swear that I was not a member of the Union League, Heroes of America* [Red Strings], *Grand Army of the Republic, or any other political organization having for its object the civil or political promotion of the colored race. I was sworn never to reveal any of the secrets of the organization which came to my knowledge…*
>
> *The meetings were to be held in secret places; in the woods, or some other place distant from any habitation, in order to avoid detection. The disguise prescribed was a long white gown, and a mask for the face. No applicant could be admitted as a member of the organization until his name had first been submitted to a regular camp…No raid was to be made, no person punished, no execution done, unless it had first been unanimously agreed upon at a regular meeting of a camp of the klan and duly approved by the officers and chief of the klan.*

There were hand signs for identification, code words for distress and a secret alphabet. Those who went on raids came from areas different from the intended victim, to lessen the chance of being identified. If called to testify against another Klansman, a member was expected to perjure himself. As far as the "trials" were concerned, an allegation of petty larceny or insulting a white woman was enough to convict and rate a nocturnal call, but according to Boyd, such accusations were usually excuses for political action—scaring prospective voters away from the polls and persuading Republican organizers to cease what they were doing. Methods were whatever the Klan thought necessary to accomplish those ends: warnings, whippings, killings.[195]

Some of North Carolina's busiest Ku Kluxers were active in Tourgee's judicial district. In July 1869, Tourgee—who had further outraged his white neighbors by adopting a mulatto child—wrote Holden that the grand jury had indicted "twenty or more" individuals on "very serious outrages," but there were many more reported "outrages" for which

> *the connection between the act and any identified persons could not be clearly, and in some of them, not at all established. In some cases the disguise was perfect, or the acts of violence were performed by strangers, so that identification was utterly impossible. In some cases the commission of the acts of violence was only revealed by accident; and in others the parties were so fearful of their lives that they begged to be permitted to refrain from testifying and in yet other circumstances they fled the country...The acts are of almost every degree of atrocity; burning houses, whipping men and women, beating with clubs, shooting, cutting and other methods of injuring and insult...I have no idea that one of these men can be legally convicted of the crime.*[196]

Former slave Caswell Holt had the distinction of being the first black deputy sheriff in Alamance County. In February 1868, white vigilantes whipped and shot him for writing the governor about bad race relations and for enforcing a curfew against whites. Another former slave, Sandy Sellars, was whipped for having the impudence to carry a white landowner's letter directing a white woman to keep her livestock out of his fields. A third former slave in Alamance County, Daniel Jordan, was called upon at home one night, chased from the house, caught and given fifty lashes for owning a horse and wagon—which the Klansmen took with them when they departed.[197]

Word of terrorism—including at least twenty-five hangings, shootings, drownings and murders by other means—came to Holden from Alamance, Chatham, Jones, Lenoir, Orange, Robeson and more counties:

> *For the space of twelve months, while the laws were thus being set at naught, and while grand juries were failing to find bills, or, if they were found, petit juries refused to convict, I was almost constantly importuned by letters, and in person, by many of the victims of these outrages, and was urged to adopt some means of protection to society, and especially to the victims of the secret combinations referred to.*
>
> *These combinations were at first purely political in their character, and many good citizens were induced to join them. But gradually, under the leadership of ambitious and discontented politicians, and under the pretext that society needed to be regulated by some authority outside or above the law, their character was changed, and these secret Klans began to commit murder, to rob, whip, scourge and mutilate unoffending citizens...Unlike other secret political associations, they authorized the use of force, with deadly weapons, to influence the elections.*[198]

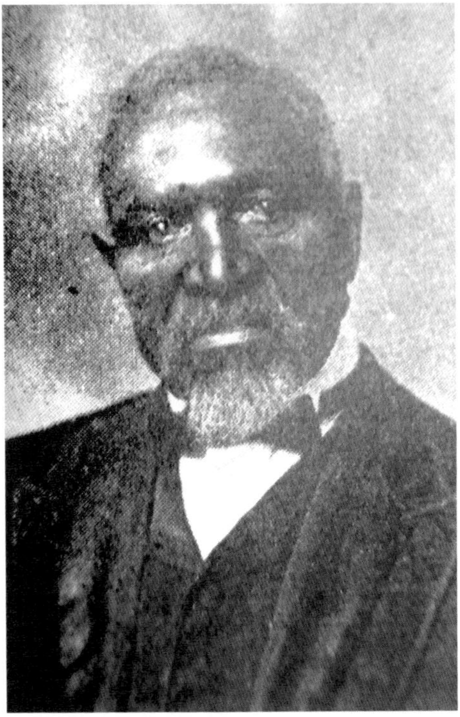

Left: Deputy Sheriff Caswell Holt was the first Ku Klux victim in Alamance County, suffering a whipping in February 1868. *From Hamilton's* History of North Carolina.

Below: "Visit of the Ku Klux," an 1872 *Harper's* illustration by Frank Belew, depicts a black home invaded by armed, masked men. *Courtesy Library of Congress.*

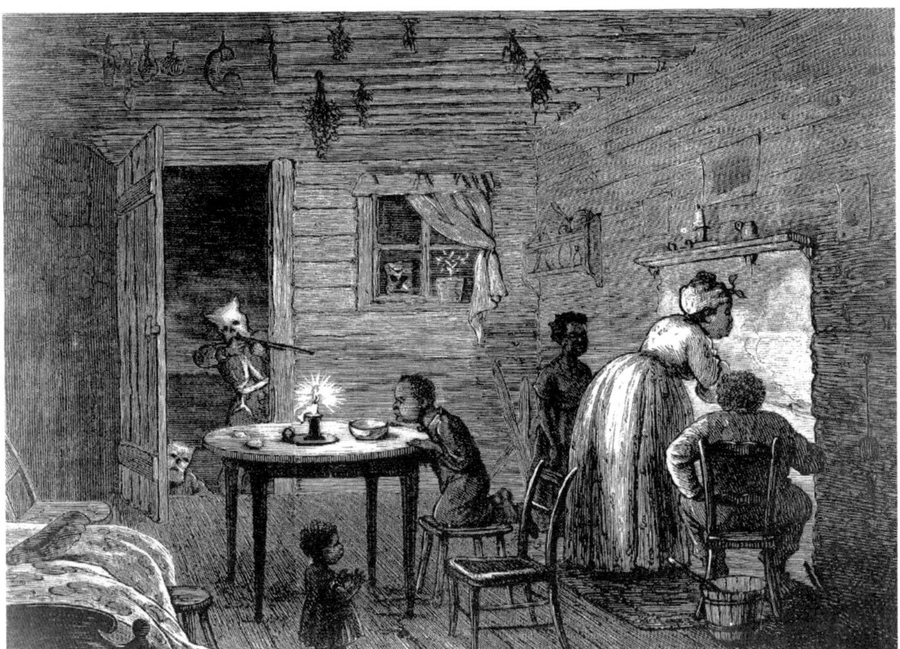

Early in 1870, the legislature gave Holden an extra weapon to fight the Klan. Introduced by Alamance Republican T.M. Shoffner, "An Act to Secure the Better Protection of Life and Property" gave the governor authority to declare a "state of insurrection" in the counties and send the militia in, whether invited or not. Shoffner was said to have received $1,200 for sponsoring the bill and would, later on, flee the state to keep his life because of it.[199] Holden was slow to make use of the "Shoffner Bill," however, thinking that he would have a hard time raising a white militia in areas so infested with night riders and their abettors, realizing that using black militia would only make things worse and knowing that the state was too close to broke to pay for an operation large and sweeping enough to be effective.

Reporting in January that arsonists had destroyed a Person County tobacco works, the *Hillsborough Recorder* wailed, probably with sarcasm, "Where is the militia bill? We thought that barn burnings, chicken and hog stealing—rapes and murders &c. were all to be stopped…Tell them to hie to Person County and find out who burnt Reams' factory, ku klux or [Union] leaguettes."[200] Instead, Holden tried working from within—enlisting men in the suffering counties who may have been Conservative Unionists but were of known good character, enjoyed the high regard of their neighbors and, maybe, had Confederate credentials and urging them to renounce violence and press the vigilantes to disband.

Some Conservatives, such as Josiah Turner, pooh-poohed reports of Ku Klux lawlessness or rationalized them as necessary measures for citizens who could not depend on the law to protect them from freedmen's and carpetbaggers' depredations. The *Recorder* claimed that there were "three outrages on the whites to one white outrage on the blacks."[201] Some others, though, were on Holden's side as far as suppressing outlawry was concerned and suggested that he should apply the same pressure he put on the Klan to the lawbreaking, allegedly incendiary Union League as well.[202]

Recognizing that he needed cooperation from the opposition party, Holden obliged by ordering the Union League to disband, along with the White Brotherhood and other bands of its ilk. In his *Memoirs*, he would describe them as "two rival secret societies" and defend his role in the league, which, he wrote,

> *was comparatively harmless, and was unarmed, and* [the Klan] *was armed. I was myself at the head of the League in this State, and the violations of law complained of were without my knowledge and against my orders. The rituals of this order were freely distributed everywhere, and*

> *those who read them will remember that they simply inculcated what was then known as loyalty, with industry, especially among the colored people, and obedience to law. The day before I took the oath of office of Governor in Capitol Square, I resigned my position as chief of the League in this State, because I could not have on my conscience my oath as Governor and at the same time an oath binding myself to a secret political society.*[203]

Holden's diplomacy had some success. In Chatham County, he recruited N.A. Ramsey, a Democrat and former captain of the Forty-first North Carolina Infantry. Ramsey went about the county speaking on the necessity of respecting the laws and keeping the peace, and meeting Klan leaders to suggest that there might be no prosecution if they stopped "ku kluxing" and might be federal occupation if they didn't. Whippings, shootings and burnings occurred less and less often in the county.

With Alexander Graham's blessing, in Orange County Holden engaged Pride Jones of Hillsborough, who told the governor that putting down the Klan by any means other than peaceable ones could only result in "a dreadful amount of blood-shed and crime."[204] Kluxers there may have been tired of the gambit, but for whatever reason they ceased and desisted, and Jones wrote Holden in April that he had been informed that the Orange County Klan was disbanded.[205]

Alamance and Caswell Counties were tougher cases. Jones offered to do what he could in Alamance, but by that time Holden had already sent in the troops.

The final straw came on February 27, when Wyatt Outlaw's body was found hanging from an elm tree less than fifty yards from the county courthouse. According to Boyd's testimony, Outlaw—the Union League organizer and a Graham town councilman—was taken from his house by a group of eighty to one hundred men and killed.

> Question: *What steps, if any, were taken to discover and bring to justice the men who were guilty of hanging that man?*
>
> Answer: *There was a coroner's jury and an inquest, and some witnesses were examined—some of the town people who saw the band in the town, and saw them take him from his house; also a negro woman, who probably lived with him. The verdict of the coroner's jury was, I believe, that he came to his death by a band of disguised men unknown.*[206]

Shoffner had already fled Klan retribution for the militia act he had sponsored, and a few days later a black man who had claimed to know who Outlaw's killers were was found in a pond where he had drowned. On March 7, Holden declared Alamance County in a state of insurrection and sent forty federal soldiers there. But the army's authority only extended to assisting local law enforcement, "and Sheriff Albert Murray did not tax them in this respect."[207] Camps in Graham and Company Shops (later Burlington) made Klan targets safer there but hardly quelled night riding in the countryside. From Alamance County, a federal officer wrote the governor:

> *The civil authorities are helpless—Squires Harding and Albright have arrested numbers and had them sent to Court, but yet not one of them was ever punished. They are now threatened with their lives, for their action and are now afraid to take any further action. After Wyatt Outlaw was murdered Henry A. Badham expressed himself rather freely about the affair and was set upon by Adolphus Moore, who is said to be a leader, badly beaten and leg broken and yet Moore is going at large... What can you do for these suffering people, a part of whom are afraid to sleep at night in their own beds. Many of whom have not slept in their homes for two months.*[208]

The Klan and/or the Conservative Party might have been using violence to pressure Holden into declaring martial law and other steps that would open him to charges of disregard for North Carolina law and outright tyranny—just the sort of charge to hit a North Carolina nerve.

> *The attacks on both Confederate authority during the war and Republican authority after it grew out of cultural patterns that had been established during the antebellum years. The war brought the common whites' egalitarian and communitarian values into sharper focus, and they responded by challenging the elites to an unprecedented extent. The eyes that had been opened by the wartime strains, began to look back with a fondness for the better times they had seen.*[209]

If so, the governor played right into their hands, though he must have felt he had little other choice. With Alamance County getting further and further out of hand, Holden wrote U.S. Grant asking him to press Congress for authority to suspend habeas corpus—for which Holden had once so thoroughly blasted Jefferson Davis—put vigilantes before military tribunals and shoot them. "We would soon have peace and order...The remedy would

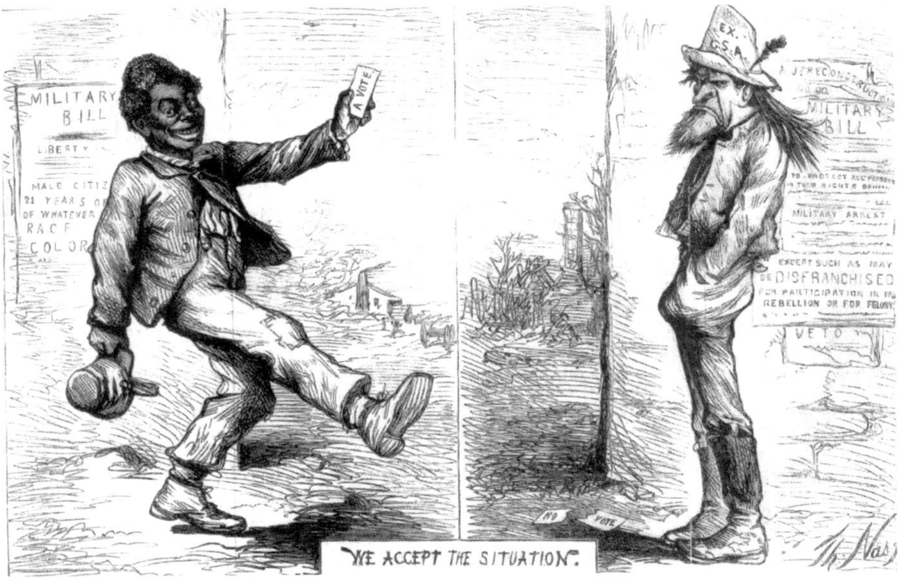

"We accept the situation," an 1867 *Harper's* illustration on Southern response to black suffrage. *Courtesy the North Carolina State Archives.*

be a short and bloody one, but it is as indispensable as was the suppression of the rebellion." He made the same request directly to his friends on Capitol Hill—"We want military tribunals by which assassins and murderers can be summarily tried and shot"—but got no encouragement for the idea.[210]

With Ku Klux shootings, burnings and threats on the upswing, freedmen hit back with raids on the homes of men they thought were night riders. Holden condemned payback in kind, which, he said, "greatly aggravates the evil, and is calculated to increase strife." In that, he was quite correct, for whatever the truth of black and Union League vandalism and arson, having the rumor in circulation and the allegations in public gave white vigilantes an excuse for their crimes and political ammunition to Conservatives hard at work to "redeem" the state in the August legislative elections. Holden's opposition already suspected that the Republicans intended to use their militant machinery to rig the elections "in order that," Josiah Turner wrote in his *Sentinel*, "they may be better enabled to rob and plunder the people and the State."[211]

Not all Conservatives were so shrill. Going into the 1870 campaigns, the party was divided into moderate and reactionary wings. Moderates were prepared to accept black voting and acknowledge blacks' civil rights and sought to rein in the party's extremists while appealing to those Republicans who had disliked Holden all along or had been embarrassed by corruption among the governor's cronies. Maybe some African American votes could be won as well, the moderates hoped. Events would work against them, though, especially as provoked by the Kluxers and reacted to by Holden.

As vigorously as anywhere in the state, rumors and allegations were swirling in Caswell County.

> *There has recently been considerable excitement in Dan River Township caused by the property of old and inoffensive citizens being burned by some scoundrels instigated by men who are as mean and devilish as the devil would have them be. On Sunday night last two Tobacco barns containing tobacco belonging to Mr. Samuel Hinton aged about 70 years living in the aforementioned township were set on fire… On Monday night after the above mentioned burning three Tobacco barns (under one roof) containing four thousand pounds fine tobacco, the property of Gen. Wm. Lea (same Township) was set on fire and entirely consumed; loss estimated between three and four thousand dollars…No one supposed he had an enemy so mean, so cowardly, as to perpetrate such a fiendish act.*[212]

And Chicken Stephens was at the storm's eye. Among the tales current about him, Stephens had told an unidentified county resident that there were five hundred Klan members in Caswell and they had to be put down by "torch." Subsequently, it was said, Stephens led a Union League rally at which the members decided to burn a number of tobacco barns; he even passed out the matches.

On a more personal level, Stephens was reputed to have murdered his own mother. Letitia Stephens had met "a very mysterious and tragic" end—as *Patriot* editor Steadman put it—having been found in her bedroom with her throat cut. Stephens himself was away from home at the time, and a coroner's inquest concluded that his mother had had a spasm and fallen down, hitting a chamber pot. The chamber pot broke, and Letitia cut herself on the sharp edge and bled to death. It does seem an unlikely scenario, and though a shard from the pot had turned up in the wound, the cut was reported as suspiciously neat.

Even his fellow Republicans, the stories went, found Stephens repugnant and wanted to get rid of him before he did any more damage to their party's reputation. When Holden contacted Caswell County resident Thomas A. Donoho about serving as his peacemaker there, Donoho advised him:

> *It is an unfortunate circumstance for the welfare of the county, as well as for the interest of your party, that the recognized exponent of the republican party in the county, should be a person of the* antecedents *and* surroundings *of the member who represents the county in the state senate.*
>
> *I do not think there would have been any violent antagonism between a respectable portion of the white people of the county and a* liberal *republicanism, but for the misrepresentation of republicanism. But the good people of Caswell cannot be expected to affiliate with a party whose recognized standard bearer sustains such a character at home, as does the individual alluded to.*[213]

Other parties had already resolved to put John Walter Stephens where he could not harm Republicans or anyone else. John Green Lea, of the old and expansive Caswell family, had been a corporal in the Third North Carolina Cavalry during the war. Back home, he organized a unit of the Ku Klux Klan, establishing a "den" in each township. Lea's sister, Ann, was the Ku Klux's seamstress, making the night riders' costumes and storing them at the family homeplace, Leahurst. The Caswell Klan's first action was whipping Jim Jones, a Tourgee appointment as justice of the peace, who had let off an accused black thief and claimed that the governor had told him to protect the rights of freedmen and he intended to do just that.

> [Jones] *says they took him out, used him roughly, and give him notice that his conduct as magistrate was such that he had better quit the business. Jones resigned as magistrate some two weeks since and left the county two or three days before the first fire occurred in the* [Dan River] *township. It is supposed the barn burning is in retaliation for the interviews held with Jones by unknown persons. What's to be the result of all this remains to be seen.*[214]

Over the course of a year or so, Lea's band whipped two whites and six blacks, shot one man and plundered some homes.[215] And then there was Stephens. Accused of directing the burning of a hotel, several stores and at least three farmers' tobacco crops, "Stephens was tried by the Ku Klux Klan and sentenced to death," Lea recorded. "He had a fair trial before a jury of twelve men." Stephens, of course, was not present at the "trial," but he had plenty of warning that his life was in danger, and he made preparations: fortifying his house, arming himself and taking out a

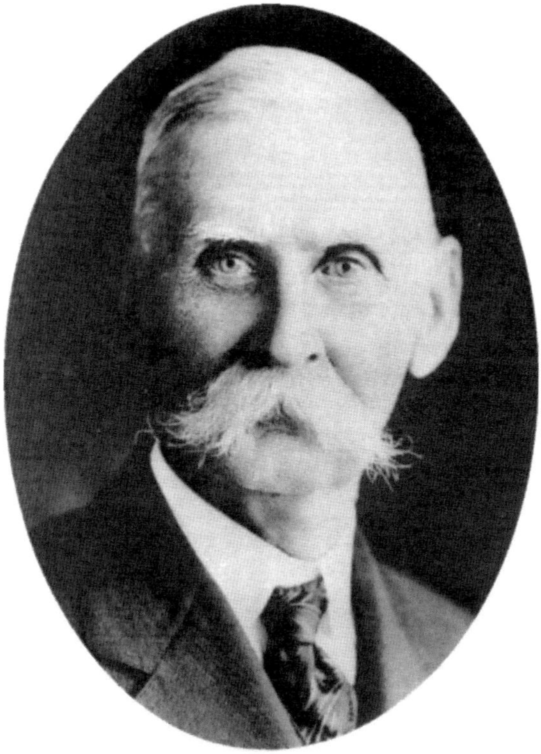

Left: John Green Lea organized the Klan in Caswell County and its conspiracy to murder scalawag John W. Stephens. *Courtesy Caswell County Historical Association.*

Below: A display of pistols, the same model as John Walter Stephens carried, at the Richmond-Miles History Museum in Yanceyville. *Rick Frederick photo, courtesy Caswell County Historical Association.*

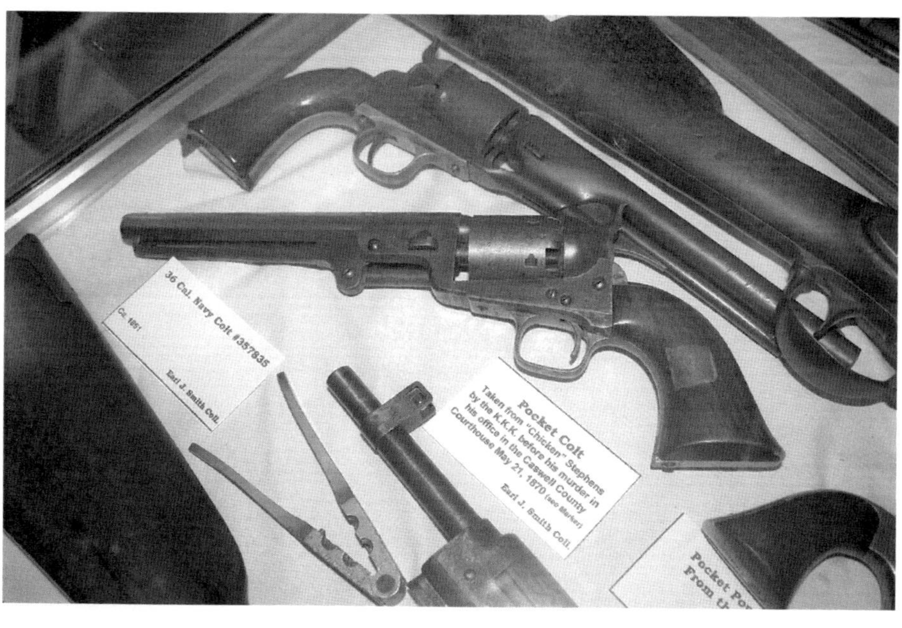

life insurance policy. He wrote Holden: "There is no use of talking about running a ticket in the next election in this County…The K.K.K. will have every thing their own way."[216]

The sentence was passed in February, but the Klan took its time carrying it out. On May 21, the Conservatives held a campaign rally at the Caswell Courthouse. Lea ordered his membership to Yanceyville for the occasion. Klansmen arrived with their robes hidden under their saddles, figuring that an opportunity would appear to carry out Stephens's execution. Stephens provided the opportunity by brazenly walking into the rally, sitting down and taking notes.

On his way into the courthouse, Stephens had stopped to talk to Frank Wiley, a former sheriff whom he was courting to run for that office again, as a Republican. Wiley told Stephens that he would have a decision for him later on, and when, after some time had passed, Wiley motioned Stephens out of the meeting room, Stephens probably figured that politics was the reason why. But Wiley was in league with the Ku Klux and luring Stephens to his death, downstairs in a back room that had been used for a Union League office. Three other men were waiting for Stephens and Wiley: James T. Mitchell, James Denny and Joseph R. Fowler. They took Stephens into the back room, shut the door and took his weapons.

Then they dithered over what to do next. Mitchell left and told Wiley he couldn't do it. Denny was left holding a pistol at Stephens's head, but he did not pull the trigger. Wiley sought Lea out and told him to do something before the plot fell apart and they were all discovered. Lea summoned several more men and rushed to the room where Stephens was being held. Lea and Stephens sat down together on a stack of firewood, and Stephens asked that his life be spared. At that point, Mitchell ran up with a rope, looped it around Stephens's neck and began to strangle him. Half a dozen others ran over, and Tom Oliver stabbed Stephens three times: once in the chest and twice in the throat. The execution carried out, the killers laid the body on the woodpile and went out. They locked the door behind them and threw the key into a creek.[217]

The Klan was rid of one scalawag, and the Conservatives would soon be rid of another.

A WAR, OF SORTS

When Stephens did not show up for supper, his wife called for his two brothers to commence a search. They gathered a party and looked all over town, including through the courthouse, but gave up when darkness fell. Resuming in the morning, one of the searchers looked through a window into the locked back room and saw the body where it had been left. The following day, Monday, May 23, speakers at a citizens' meeting denounced the murder "and all kindred acts of violence and lawlessness who whomsoever, wherever and for whatever end perpetrated." One E.B. Withers "foreshadowed and delineated the direful and calamitous consequences, which…would inevitably attend a course of such reckless and total disregard of human law."

The citizens approved a resolution condemning and deploring the murder, counseling moderation and restraint of "evil passions" and calling for apprehension of those responsible and to end the actions of "secret oath-bound associations."[218] A subsequent inquest concluded that there had been murder but left the perpetrators "unknown." Sheriff Jesse Griffith did not exert himself to solve the case, and state representative Wilson Carey, an African American Republican, hurried across the county line.[219] Rumors went about that Stephens's assassins had been Union Leaguers out to pin a dastardly crime on the Ku Klux.[220]

Tourgee wrote a friend:

> *Another brave, honest Republican citizen has met his fate at the hands of these fiends. Warned of his danger, and fully cognizant of the terrible risk*

> *which surrounded him, he still manfully refused to quit the field. Against the advice of his friends, against the entreaties of his family, he constantly refused to leave those who had stood by him in the day of his disgrace and peril. He was accustomed to say that 3,000 poor, ignorant, colored Republican voters in that county had stood by him and elected him, at the risk of persecution and starvation, and that he had no idea of abandoning them to the Ku-Klux. He was determined to stay with them, and either put an end to these outrages, or die with the other victims of Rebel hate and national apathy.*[221]

Martial law in Alamance County had had limited success. Holden's overture toward Caswell had been rebuffed, Donoho assuring him that people there had no interest in politics and were rather devoted to "repair[ing] their shattered fortunes and build[ing] up their waste places" while maintaining harmony between the races. The Klan was clearly out of control, the Conservatives were getting more and more strident in their criticisms and elections were not far off. For Holden, the situation was close to desperate, and after a strategy session with his advisors in the wake of Stephens's murder, he decided to call out more troops.

He also wanted to make sure that he had support in Washington. Holden wrote to the president, and Grant replied by asking why Holden had not led the troops in himself, before now. Grant also gave his opinion that North Carolina law gave Holden all the authority he needed to put disorders down and assured the governor that, if he needed them, federal troops would be on the way. Grant also directed the War Department to provide the impoverished state government with the gear it would need to go on the offensive.[222]

Holden and his colleagues started by organizing two regiments of state militia, recruiting white soldiers from outside their theaters of operation. For one, the governor engaged William J. Clarke, a state comptroller before the war and colonel of the Twenty-fourth North Carolina during the war. Thirty-four years before, Clarke had been one of the students with whom Holden shared the coach on his way to Raleigh; by 1870, he was a well-established lawyer and businessman in New Bern and, ironically enough, although a loyal Republican, was married to a sister-in-law of Josiah Turner.[223]

With one commander from the eastern part of the state, Holden wanted the other from the west, where Union loyalty had always been high and mountain men had fought on the federal side. For whatever reason, he first asked Wallace W. Rollins, who had actually fought on both sides. Rollins turned him down, and Holden then approached George W. Kirk, who accepted the commission, though it was not the most politic appointment the governor could have made.

After Sherman, Kirk was arguably the Yankee most despised in North Carolina for depredations on civilians during the war. Actually a Tennessean, by birth and residence, Kirk became an officer in a Union mounted infantry unit in Knoxville and rode with it into western North Carolina to promote the Northern cause, attack Rebel interests, aid deserters and escaped slaves and do some looting here and there. By 1864, he had his own command, the Third North Carolina Mounted Infantry, or "Kirk's Raiders." From a base in Tennessee, Kirk's two thousand soldiers earned a reputation for brutality as they killed, commandeered and burned through the high country and foothill towns.[224]

> *It was the intention of these outlaws to waste our wheat fields, in order, if possible, to starve the people into submission to the hated and detested government of Abe Lincoln. Who but savages, yes, worse than savages, resort to such a mode of warfare? The history of the world does not contain an instance when it has been done.*[225]

In Hillsborough, even the relatively moderate *Recorder* questioned Holden's judgment in picking Kirk for command:

> *Bearing such a reputation among a large class of our people as Col. Kirk does, (even though he doesn't deserve it) we think it unproductive of peace and good feeling to mount him with sword in hand and march him to put down ruptures between* [Union] *league and ku klux—to restore "peace"—whose reputation itself goes before him at "war" with prejudices that lay now like dead ashes but that need only the name and appearance of this man among them to kindle the more living coals afresh.*[226]

"Cut-throat Kirk," as he was known in Alamance County, began raising his command as soon as his commission was official on June 20. To help recruiting, the *Standard*'s print shop had given him five hundred posters proclaiming: "The horrible murders and other atrocities committed by rebel K.K.K. and 'Southern chivalry' on grayhaired men and helpless women, call in thunder tones on all loyal men to rally in defense of their state. The uplifted hands of justice must overtake these outlaws."

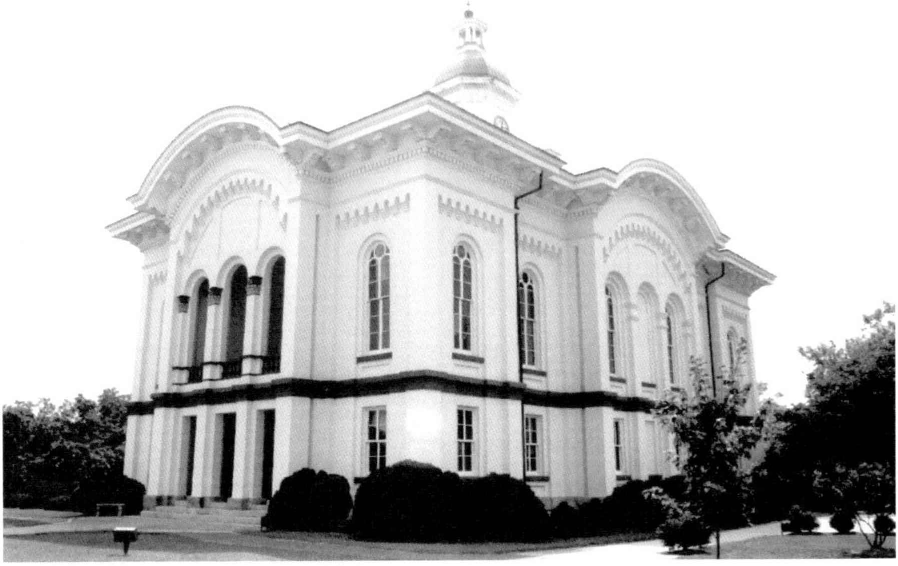

The courthouse in Yanceyville, where John W. Stephens died and Colonel Kirk broke up a political rally. *Author's photo.*

The posters also offered the same clothes, food and pay as that the regular U.S. troops got, in exchange for six months' active duty. Barnstorming east Tennessee as well as western North Carolina, Kirk managed to enlist 670 men, though he had sought 1,000. The recruits' ages ranged from fifteen to more than sixty, and their lack of discipline and generally rowdy behavior left bad impressions in the towns where they mustered before boarding trains for Alamance County, where Tourgee was holding court despite multiple warnings that he was destined for a fate like Stephens's. Kirk's men occupied the county courthouse and proceeded to arrest the men on a list the governor had given him. There were a few instances of prisoners being "mistreated," as Kirk acknowledged at the U.S. Senate hearings: a zealous officer had choked men to get information about the Wyatt Outlaw murder, but reports of others being hung up by their thumbs were denied by Kirk.[227]

On July 15, Kirk and his men set out for Caswell, which Holden had declared a week earlier to be also in a state of insurrection. On the way, they encountered John A. Pinnix, a physician on his way to a political rally in Yanceyville. Pinnix was immediately arrested, no reason given, and ordered to come along with the troops. Up ahead, he saw a wagon carrying two men he knew from Alamance County. The doctor lagged while soldiers "clad in bright new uniforms, carrying shining muskets, bearing flaunting flags" trooped right past him; he then took his chance to make a break for it.

Arriving in Yanceyville before Kirk, Pinnix warned the citizens that they were being invaded. A big crowd was waiting, "unafraid and determined," Pinnix later wrote, on the town common outside the courthouse where the rally was going on. Kirk arrived, surrounded the building and sent soldiers dashing inside. The crowd heard a pistol fired, and then "the wildest pandemonium followed. Men struggled with each other to get out of the building, only to be halted on the stairways by the sharp point of murderous bayonets." Hearing the commotion, a federal unit camped nearby moved in to see what was going on. As soon as they were noticed, Kirk's militia began behaving in a more orderly fashion to carry out the arrests Holden had ordered.

After scouring the courthouse and settling in for the duration, Kirk sent squads into the countryside. One of their first apprehensions there was Frank Wiley, whom they came upon as he was plowing his tobacco. When Wiley asked what he was charged with, the soldiers swore at him; when he demanded a chance to see his lawyer, they knocked him down with a fence rail and ordered him to get up on the horse they had unhitched from Wiley's plow. His hands tied, the former sheriff was then escorted to town with militiamen switching him with hickory sticks along the way.[228]

John Green Lea escaped arrest at the courthouse, but the following day as he was taking a nap his sister brought him news that ten or twelve soldiers were in the yard. Lea went to get his pistols, but the sister dissuaded him and he went peaceably along to Yanceyville with only a single guard who rode an aged horse.

> *The soldier that carried me begged me all the way to Yanceyville not to let anybody shoot him. He also…begged me to let him come to my house and work for me, saying he did not expect to find as many kind people and that he would be glad to live in the neighborhood; that he had been brought down from the mountains, not knowing where he was going nor what he was to do, or what sort of people he would be among. When Kirk's men arrived in Yanceyville, old Aunt Willie Lee was selling ice cream at the courthouse. It was the first they had ever seen and several* [of] *them said, "Ain't his the best frozen victuals you ever taste?"*[229]

The Conservative press attacked Holden for commissioning Kirk, "a guerilla bandit from East Tennessee," and for using his military authority

FACTS FOR THE PEOPLE

To Read, Ponder and Digest, if they can.

For the benefit of those who really desire information, and to show in proper light the Extravagance, Wastefulness, and utter disregard for the people's best interests, shown by the Radical party, we submit the following comparison of the expense of one year of Democratic rule, under Gov. Bragg in 1857 & '58; and one year ending Sept. 30th, 1869, under the Radical rule of William W. Holden:

	Expenditures 1857, '58.	Expenditures 1868, '69.
Adjutant General,	$ 200 00	$ 1965 56
Capitol Square.	1277 82	3687 73
Executive Department,	2550 00	7752 65
Treasury Department,	2750 00	6082 96
Keeper of Capitol,	266 00	1054 19
Auditor's Department,	1000 00	4010 54
Binding Laws,	1073 25	6596 96
Copying Laws,	348 50	1608 60
State Department,	800 00	3903 25
Public Printing,	5240 57	28,685 10
Judiciary,	28,163 15	54,130 50
General Assembly,	49,113 54	191,102 10
Fugitives from Justice,	572 75	6,834 00

Contingences for 1868, '69, $76,506 64

☛ Among the expenditures for 1868, '69, may be found such items as these:—

). D. Colgrove, one copy of "How to Make the Farm pay,"	$ 4 50
D. Wilkie, Holden's detective,	1042 90
H. Mowers, " "	949 75
tate Militia, (to outrage Jones County,)	1864 91
ewbern Republican, for adv. duties S. C. C.,	250 00
ewbern Times, printing Badges for Militia,	18 80
Douglass Bell, for Toilet Soap,	6 00
Geo. W. Nason, jr., Drawer locks, Chairs and Water Coolers,	130 20
Phil. Thiem, 6 Baskets, 1 Corkscrew,	9 00
Half doz. ostrich feathers, water bucket and dipper,	16 75

OTHER FACTS FOR THE CITIZENS OF CRAVEN COUNTY ESPECIALLY.

The entire tax for this County levied for all purposes in 1867, under a Democratic State Government was $18,000. This, deducting the tax on Polls, was only 3-4 of one per cent on the assessed value of property.

The tax for this year, under Radical rule, will reach $47,000. Deduct the Poll tax and the tax levied on real and personal property as assessed, will reach 2 1-2 per cent.

Citizens of Craven, how like you this picture of increase in the short space of two years?

Again—It is a fact worthy of note, that the principal officials, County Commissioners, Legal Adviser of the Board, (R. F. Lehman, Esq., $500,) have all been paid dollar for dollar of their claims, while the jurors, witnesses, &c., have their tickets on hand, or have been subjected to a shave of seventy *per cent.* to get the money for them.

☛ This is Radical justice—Radical love and care for the poor white and colored man, with a vengeance!

☛ Next week we will show you other iniquities of the party in power. ☚

"Facts for the People," an 1870 Conservative campaign poster listing misdeeds of William Holden's administration. *Courtesy the North Carolina State Archives.*

"to overawe and terrify the people" to the Republican Party's benefit. Josiah Turner dared Holden to have him arrested for defending Klan action in his *Sentinel* and, after claiming that someone had fired a shot into his Hillsborough house, spurned a request for details from Holden's secretary. Holden ordered twenty militiamen to guard Turner's home. Turner replied that he would have the guards arrested for trespassing; Holden suggested publicly that Turner had made up the gunshot story.

Kirk, who had expected armed resistance, was spooked by reports of Ku Kluxers near Yanceyville to the point that he feared attack by five thousand insurgents and asked Holden to send reinforcements and artillery. No attack came, the arrests went along with little disturbance and within a week or two about one hundred citizens were in custody awaiting military trials. A federal officer reported bad behavior by Kirk's men, raiding farms and treating local whites with considerable disdain, threatening people and scattering the county records in the streets of Yanceyville. The county's sense of decency was outraged when one of Kirk's mountain men stripped and took a bath in a public fountain.

Holden himself made a serious miscalculation. Almost immediately after arrests began in Alamance County, the prisoners' lawyers petitioned Chief Justice Richmond Pearson—the man who had sworn Holden into office two years before and had advised Conservatives to vote for U.S. Grant to avoid provoking the Washington Radicals—for a writ of habeas corpus. The attorneys included William A. Graham and Augustus Merrimon, and Pearson issued the writ, requiring that the arrested men be brought before him for his decision whether they were being held for just cause. Kirk refused to obey, claiming that the prisoners were to come before a military tribunal. The lawyers then asked Pearson for an order to have Kirk arrested and brought, with the prisoners, for hearing in Raleigh.[230]

Holden intervened, informing the judge that Kirk had acted upon his orders, and that he was within his authority:

> *For months past there has been maturing in* [Alamance and Caswell Counties] *under the guidance of bad and disloyal men, a dangerous secret insurrection…To the majority of the people of these sections the approach of night is like death; the men dare not sleep beneath their roofs at night, but abandoning their wives and little ones wander in the woods until day. Thus civil government was crumbling around me. I determined to nip this new treason in the bud.*[231]

When he made his ruling, Pearson approved Holden's use of the military but denied his right to suspend habeas corpus and refused to order Kirk's arrest for fear of galvanizing the insurgents into action against the militia. Holden, though, refused to produce the prisoners: "It would be a mockery in me to declare that the civil authority was unable to protect the citizens against the insurgents, and then turn the insurgents over to the civil authority." The standoff went on, even as election day drew near.

Holden would always deny that he had political motives in enrolling the two militia regiments, and he had indeed resisted pleas from party members to hold off until after the election and to pick someone other than Kirk for one of his commanders. Conservatives took his disclaimers as typical Holden; Turner just called him a liar in print. Holden ordered some of Kirk's militia to Cleveland County "to keep an eye on Plato Durham," the Conservative who had distinguished himself at the constitutional convention, and to other counties to quell any excitement during the August 4 election.

The election did go off in peace, and Republicans lost in a landslide. The Conservative William Shipp defeated the Republican Samuel Phillips for attorney general, the only state office on the ballots. Conservatives won five of the state's seven congressional seats and control of the General Assembly. Both sides were surprised at the outcome. While Republicans held on to some legislative seats in the east, where there were large black populations, their strength in the Piedmont and west was all but gone. Holden's own party quickly turned against its governor, blaming his "military experiment," the railroad scandals, taxes increased to meet the crushing state debt—all were Holden's doing, and Holden's doing had brought the party down. On the Conservative side, almost as soon as the votes were counted, a cry went up for the governor to be impeached.[232]

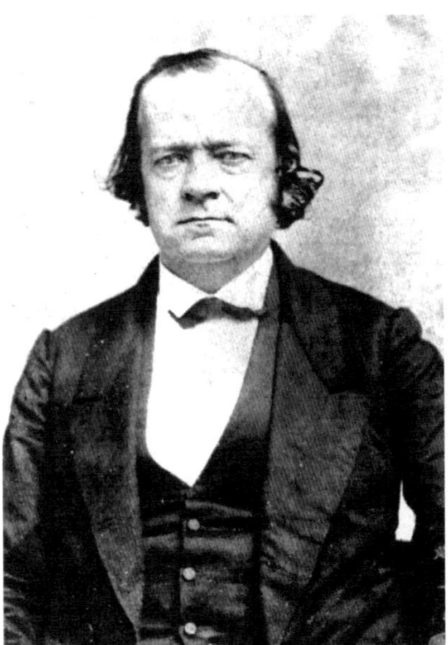

Josiah Turner of Hillsborough dared Holden to arrest him for supporting the Klan. Holden obliged. Bad mistake. *Courtesy the North Carolina State Archives.*

The governor was only going to make things worse for himself. Before the election results were known, he had Josiah Turner arrested and taken to the Yanceyville courthouse—which he referred to as a "Holden's Basteil." Dubbed "King of the Ku Klux," though he was not—publicly at least—a member, Turner repeatedly defied Holden, toured the state making inflammatory speeches calculated to set citizens and militia against one another and repeatedly dared the governor to arrest him. On August 3, he published an open letter to Holden in the *Sentinel*: "You say you will handle me in due time. You white-livered recreant, do it now. You dare me to resist you; I dare you to arrest me…Your ignorant Jacobins are incited…by your lying charges against me that I am King of the ku Klux. You villain, come and arrest a man."

Turner signed the letter "with contempt and defiance."[233] This time, the administration took the dare, though Holden would always disclaim responsibility. Colonel George Bergen, the man Kirk acknowledged to have abused prisoners during interrogation, arrested Turner at his home in Hillsborough—notwithstanding that Orange County was not under martial law.

While Turner had been baiting the governor, the Conservative attorneys had turned their attention to federal judge George Washington Brooks in Salisbury. They appealed to Brooks to take over their clients' cases as denials of civil rights. Brooks, though he had supported Holden during the war and received his job by Holden's appointment, agreed, reasoning that the same Fourteenth Amendment the Conservatives had so despised forbade a state to "deprive any person of life, liberty, or property, without due process of law," and an 1867 state law empowered federal courts to issue writs of habeas corpus when constitutional liberties might be at risk.

Stunned again, Brooks's decision coming hard upon the election returns, Holden appealed to U.S. Grant for backing when he refused to honor Brooks's writ. Grant, staunch as he had been previously on Holden's behalf, now sought legal advice. The attorney general, Amos Ackerman, said that Brooks was acting legally and advised Holden to comply. Brooks heard some of the cases himself and dismissed them for lack of evidence. The rest of the prisoners went before Judge Pearson, who released all but three. No one was ever convicted for any alleged Ku Klux crime in Alamance or Caswell County.

In September, Holden disbanded the militia he had called up and declared the state of insurrection over. The militia's presence had quieted the Ku Klux and sent some members into exile out of state. But the election had sealed the Klan's victory, so its job was done anyway. The freed prisoners went home to celebrations, none grander than that accorded Turner upon his return to Raleigh. Flush with success, both electoral and legal, Conservative lawyers sought the arrests of Kirk, Bergen and other militia officers. Brooks heard their arguments but eventually dismissed the case. Wake County authorities spirited Kirk and Bergen out of town before they were seized by a waiting mob. The lawyers even applied for Holden's arrest, on a charge of Turner's illegal arrest. The state supreme court ruled that the governor was not subject to arrest. Its decision read, in part: "The Court holds that a Court of Impeachment is the proper tribunal to try abuses of Executive authority."[234]

And so it was to be.

REPRISALS AND REDEMPTIONS

Not all Conservatives were intent on Holden's impeachment. William J. Yates, in the *Western Democrat* of Charlotte, advised taking care not to provoke the governor and his associates to pull Congress in to reconstruct North Carolina still further, and former governor Zeb Vance, among others, warned against alarming blacks that their voting rights were about to be taken away. But again, the voices of passion were louder, blood was in the water and the opposition party was in control at the state Capitol. If they could depose Holden, they calculated, the Republican organization would wither and die.[235]

The governor tried to seize the initiative, requesting county statistics on murders, whippings and other crimes of person thought due to the Klan in the past two years. His friends at the *Standard* defended his handling of the Klan situation in an editorial:

> *A few months ago the State was torn with internal dissentions. Bands of men, masked and armed, rose throughout fields and forests. They swept through our villages and rent the night with savage outcries. They held midnight gatherings in the woods, and pledged themselves to hostility to the colored race and to the Republican party, with blasphemous oaths...No conscience, no fear of Almighty God, no human compassion, no terrors of civil law, no outraged public sentiment, not even the shrieks of unoffending womanhood nor the death agonies of innocent men withheld them from the consummation of their deeds of violence and blood...*

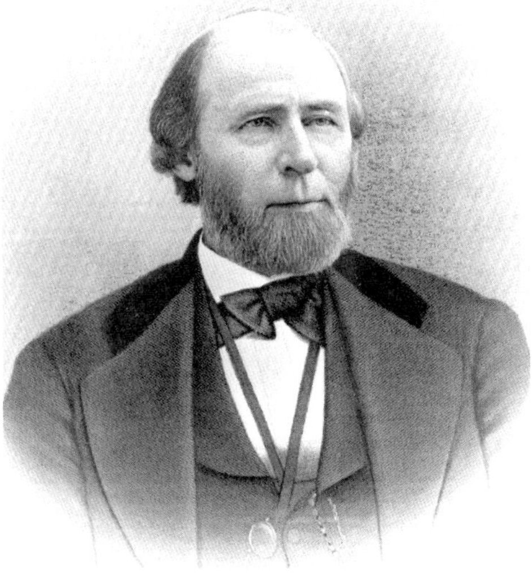

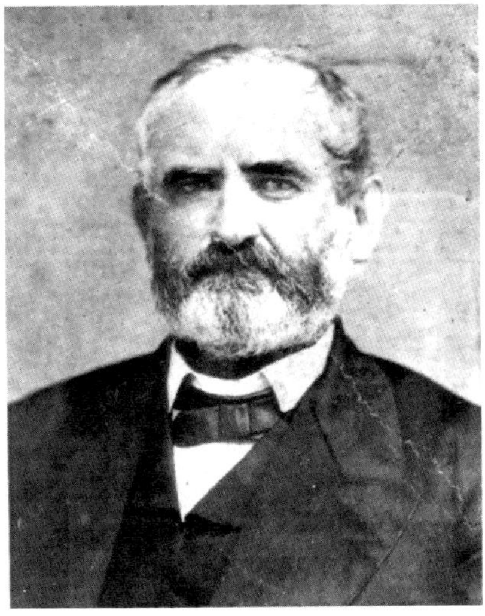

Above, left: North Carolina governor William Woods Holden. Formal portrait. *Courtesy the North Carolina State Archives.*

Above, right: Lieutenant Governor Todd R. Caldwell took over the governorship when Holden was impeached in December 1870. *Courtesy the North Carolina State Archives.*

> *One man held the power to crush these crimes, and that man was the Governor…Where before there was terror, disorder and crime, there now is security, order and peace…The more honor is due to Gov. Holden for his unflinching discharge of his duty.*[236]

When the new legislature convened in November, Holden tried to strike a friendly tone. He admitted that his administration had failed to meet its goals in education, railroad building and other areas, due to lack of money, and he admitted that the state had issued too many railroad bonds at the same time. He spoke about the night riders and their criminal activity and told the assembly that he had restored law and order to the point he could rescind his insurrection decrees. He exhorted the legislators to set partisan bitterness aside and cooperate with him in the interests of prosperity, but not even threats of a U.S. Senate investigation into North Carolina outrages could keep the Conservatives from bringing the governor to trial. On December 19, the House adopted by a vote of sixty to forty-six a resolution of impeachment on eight counts, including unlawfully sending troops into Alamance and Caswell Counties, refusing to obey writs of habeas corpus and illegally arresting Turner.

It was an almost unprecedented act. While a president, Andrew Johnson, had been impeached by Congress, only one governor—Charles Robinson of Kansas—had been brought before a legislature to face removal from his office. Robinson, like Johnson, had been acquitted. The charges against Holden included nothing regarding the railroad bond scandals, in part because nothing directly implicated the governor and in part because his alleged abuse of power and of constitutional rights involved principles closer to the state's traditional ideological heart.

As soon as the House approved its articles of impeachment, Holden was obliged to turn the state over to Lieutenant Governor Todd R. Caldwell. He did so at two o'clock on the afternoon of December 20, and not long afterward he had himself baptized at Raleigh's First Baptist Church, telling the congregation, "I have done a great deal of wrong in my life, but I will, with Heaven's help, endeavor to do better hereafter." Some of the Northern press found the embattled sinner's piety amusing, while one First Baptist member, a story goes, advised the pastor to immerse the repentant executive in lye.[237]

Holden later insisted:

> *The whole proceeding on the part of the State against the respondent was thoroughly partisan. The counsel for the State pressed the charges against me with as much particularity and vehemency as they would have done had I been arraigned for murder. I have read all their speeches, all their remarks throughout the whole proceedings, all their examination of the witnesses; and I here and now declare with the utmost solemnity, that I am not guilty of the charges preferred against me, and ought to have been acquitted on all of the eight as I was on the first two. There is no person so well qualified to say I am not guilty as myself. I* know *I am not guilty.*[238]

With the Senate still examining members' credentials to ensure a two-thirds Conservative majority, Holden's trial got underway on January 30. Pearson presided, and the governor's lawyers won some points, notably Pearson's ruling that the defense could introduce evidence of Ku Klux atrocities to demonstrate that Alamance and Caswell Counties had been legally in a state of insurrection. The prosecution's attorneys—among them Graham, Merrimon and former governor Thomas Bragg—contended that "insurrection" could only be interpreted as rebellion against the national government, but the Shoffner Act was broad enough to include any condition of criminal activity that local authorities could not suppress. The judge's decision proved a mixed blessing for Holden, though, since it also opened the way for prosecution evidence of unlawful arrests.

Holden's interest also prevailed when some Conservatives tried, with proceedings already in progress, to introduce a ninth impeachment article: conspiring with George Swepson to defraud the state by manipulating the railroad bonds. Merrimon, hoodwinked by Swepson's scam, prepared the article, but the prosecution dropped the whole idea once cooler heads reminded those behind it that defense testimony would implicate many of those legislators counted on for Holden's conviction—maybe even Merrimon himself. The danger was made clear when Swepson, from safety out of state, wired a promise that, if the article were introduced, he would "divulge everything I know." "I know what members of the General Assembly have been paid; I don't pretend to know every one of them, but enough to cause dismay. I know all the Railroad Presidents who have paid to get their bills through."[239]

During the trial, 61 witnesses appeared for the prosecution, 113 for the defense. At first, Holden came to observe his trial each day. When Josiah Turner testified, though, he was asked his own feelings toward the defendant and replied that they were those "a good man would have for a bad man." Holden stood and objected and, before Pearson could tell him he was out of order, walked out and did not return.

Instead, Holden went to Washington, possibly to put himself out of harm's way from the Klan and definitely to lobby Congress and Grant to intervene in North Carolina. He got no encouragement of federal action on his own behalf but was in town when Grant asked for "severe laws" to strike at the Ku Klux and for the congressional debate that followed. He was still in the capital when the North Carolina Senate convicted him on six of the eight counts. He was acquitted on the charges regarding his declarations of insurrection but found guilty of illegally recruiting Tennesseans to serve in North Carolina's militia, of unlawful arrests and of violating habeas corpus. The senate immediately put Holden out of office, and Turner was almost as quick to file suit against the now-former governor for damages due to his arrest.[240]

Never before had a state tried and deposed a sitting governor, but as a precedent had been set, others quickly followed: later in 1871, Nebraska ousted David Butler; in 1872, Louisiana's Henry Warmoth was suspended from the governorship pending an impeachment trial that never took place; and in 1876, Adelbert Ames resigned with impeachment proceedings underway in Mississippi. The latter two were Reconstruction Republicans.

Holden made plenty of enemies in his twisting political career and created questions in the public mind about his motives and character that would never be fully answered. He was a politician gifted enough to rise high in four parties and, through one try after another, maneuver himself into the governor's chair by popular vote. But he was also cocky, myopic and/or so out of touch with his state after two years in office that he would blunder himself out—first by blithely going along with the bond schemes and attributing any reports of misdoing to politics and then by picking an inopportune moment to strike at the Ku Klux Klan and going on to overstep his authority—perhaps letting his temper get the better of his judgment.

Holden also took much down with him. Although the Republicans would regain control of the legislature in 1872, their machine was crippled and could not hold on to power. North Carolina remained a lively, partisan scene for decades, with the eastern Second Congressional District earning the nickname "Black Second" for the African American dominance of its politics. But racial attitudes and practices were hardening into the form that resulted in Jim Crow laws and blacks' removal from electoral politics after Democrats crushed a Populist/Republican surge in 1898.

His two years in office, and the spectacle of his impeachment, had some results about which Holden and his party could only feel satisfaction. Holden was still in Washington when Congress passed the "Force Bill," giving the president authority to suspend habeas corpus and use federal troops to suppress armed groups practicing terror tactics and other Klan-like acts. Using the bill's provisions, the U.S. government rounded up scores of Klansmen, mostly in South Carolina, tried and convicted them. Congress also conducted hearings on Klan organization and atrocities that made its career familiar nationwide.

Still, in North Carolina, for practical purposes Reconstruction was over. By killing John Walter Stephens, John G. Lea and the Caswell Klan set off Holden's second declaration of insurgency, brought the infamous George Kirk back into action and solidified a case for the governor's impeachment and removal. Lea and his associates had one enemy in mind but, with his murder, unknowingly brought down the whole establishment they opposed and set the stage for a century of delay before Reconstruction's agenda for African Americans was accomplished.

Holden stayed on in Washington for a while, plagued by lawsuits at home and worried about his own future. He turned to his Republican friends, including Grant, in hopes of landing a government job. No offers came, the national party finding his name and reputation a political liability in

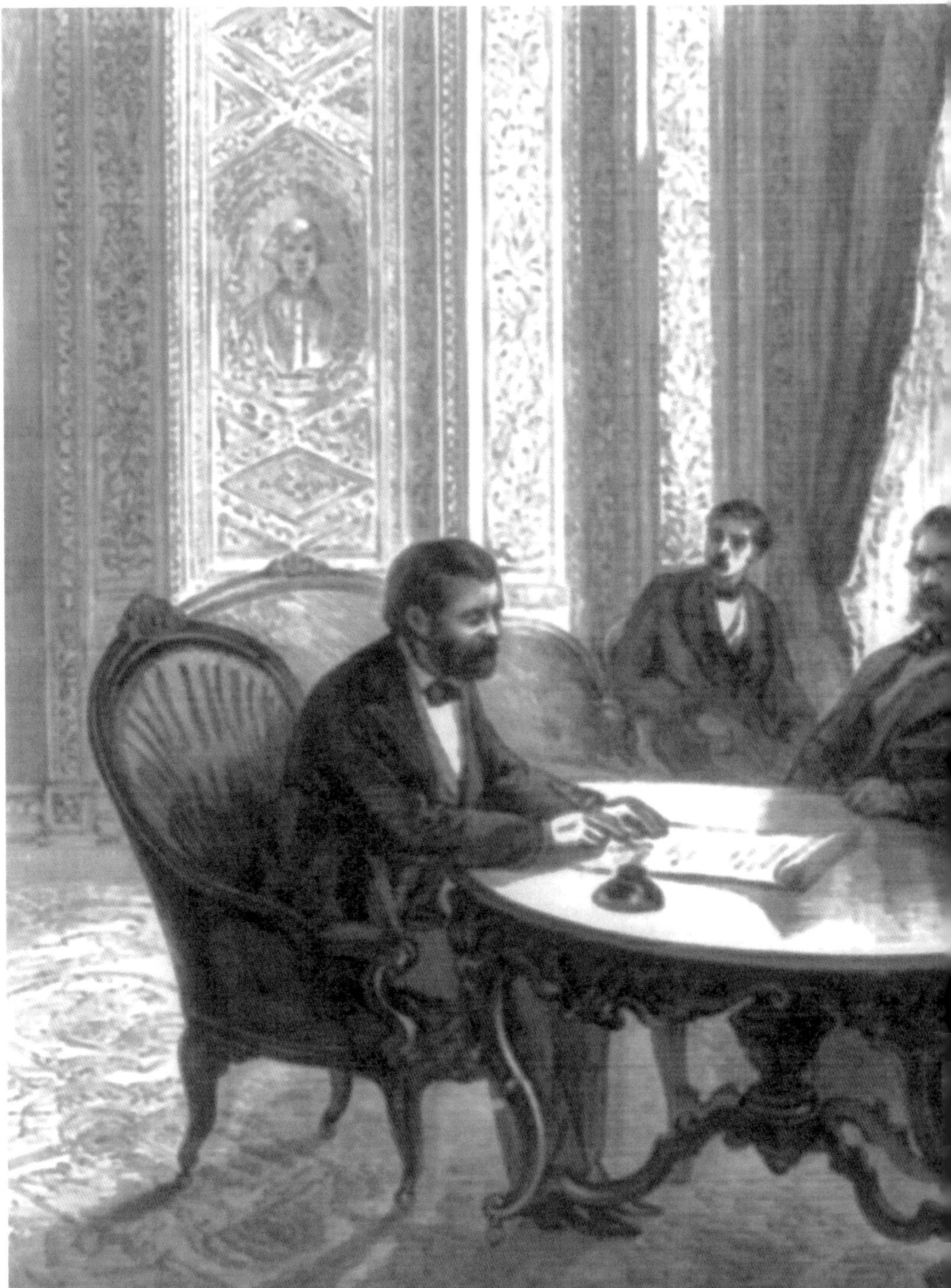

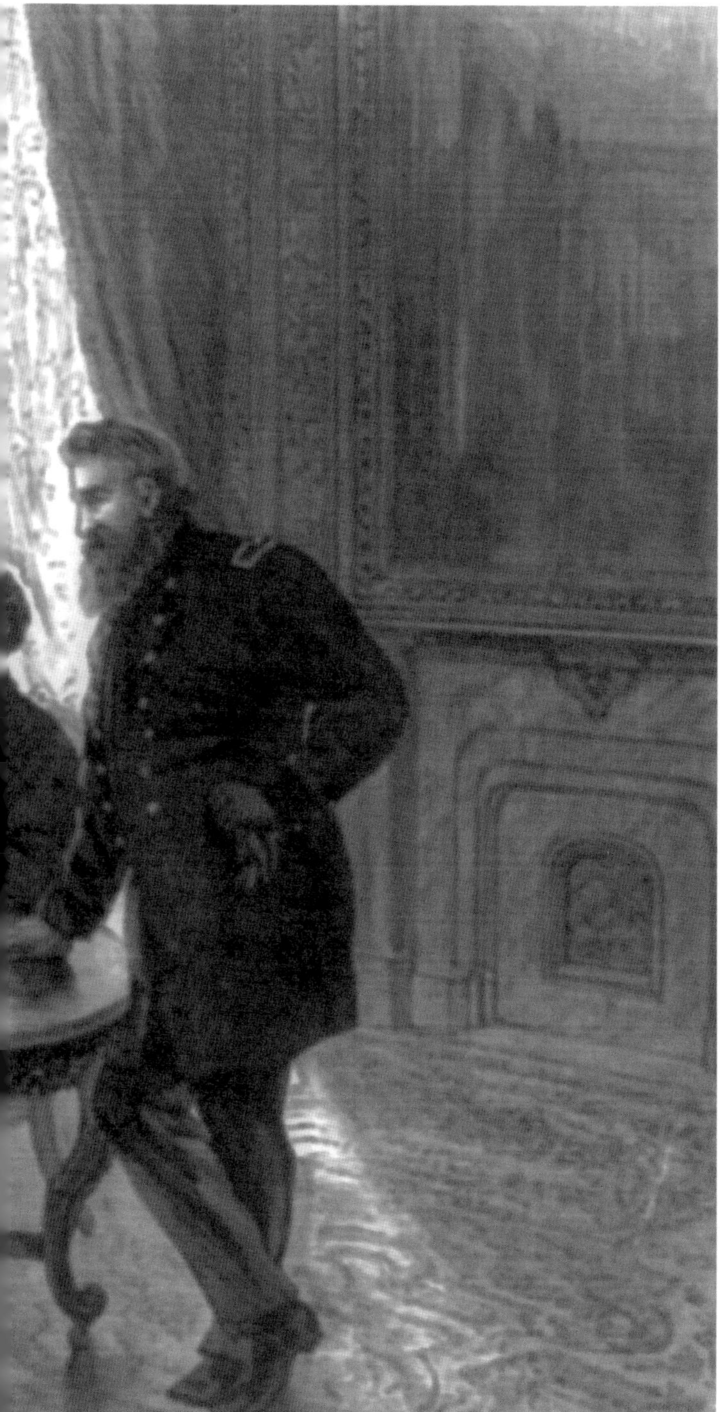

President Ulysses S. Grant signs the "Force Bill" aimed at curbing the Ku Klux Klan in the spring of 1871. Federal intervention led to Kluxers' arrests and convictions. *Courtesy Library of Congress.*

light of his transgressions against civil liberties. After some months, he was offered an editor's job at the Republican Party newspaper, which he accepted. He used the position to rail against the Ku Klux and cheer on the federal officials responsible for enforcing the Force Bill. After two years' exile, Holden returned to Raleigh, having put much of his assets into his wife's name to protect them from civil actions.

Grant gave him a job as Raleigh's postmaster. He dabbled in politics, receiving a resolution of thanks for his labor against the Klan from the state Republican convention in 1872, but kept behind the scenes to avoid giving Conservatives—later, Democrats—an easy target. In 1873, he opposed prosecution of fifteen Alamance County men in connection with Wyatt Outlaw's lynching:

> *Those crimes were not committed in ordinary times. There was a formidable and for a time an all controlling insurrection. There was a government within the government. The civil magistrate was powerless. Military power was invoked. The Ku Klux organization was disbanded. Order was restored. I do not deem it advisable to deal with offenses committed under such conditions in the ordinary way. I am in favor of amnesty, oblivion, mercy to the guilty.*[241]

Holden took his last political misstep in 1880, when he supported Grant's unsuccessful campaign against James Garfield for the Republican presidential nomination. After Garfield was elected, Holden lost his postmaster job and publicly renounced the Republican Party, claiming that it was biased against the South and had embraced the idea of black equality. Crippled by strokes, he never got around to writing a Reconstruction history from his own point of view, only completing his self-defensive *Memoirs* before his death on March 2, 1892. He was seventy-four years old, and when he died another of Josiah Turner's lawsuits was still in process against him.[242]

Albion Tourgee held out in North Carolina until 1878, although Emma, weary of the hostilities and pressures in the South and wanting peaceful surroundings in which to raise their family, moved to Erie, Pennsylvania. Albion served out his term as judge, leaving the post in 1874 and looking for a job around Greensboro until Grant made him a pension officer in Raleigh. Four years later, he left, having reconciled with Emma, and settled down to a writing career in Erie. His first novel, *A Fool's Errand by One of the Fools*, a thinly fictionalized account of his Southern experience, was a bestseller. He moved to New York, became a literary celebrity and an advocate for black

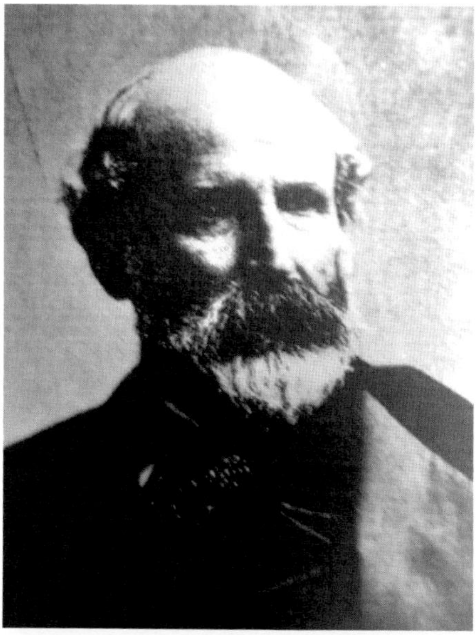

Left: Former state legislator Matthew Ransom defended George Swepson when he was arrested for the railroad bond fraud. *Courtesy the North Carolina State Archives.*

Below: John Walter Stephens's gravestone describes him as a soldier and a patriot, but ironically on the Confederate side. *Author's photo.*

rights and then came out of legal retirement to argue the plaintiff's side before the Supreme Court in *Plessy v. Ferguson*. Tourgee and Plessy, holding that discriminatory seating on railroad cars was a civil rights violation, lost the case, and a standard was set for subsequent "separate-but-equal" laws.

George Swepson was indicted for his frauds in 1870 and arrested in 1871. Merrimon and Matthew Ransom, a former North Carolina attorney general and legislator, served as his counsel, and he was never prosecuted. He and Milton Littlefield went on to perpetrate another railroad fraud in Florida, though eventually they did make some restitution to the Western North Carolina Railroad.[243]

Josiah Turner's friends gradually turned against him. Bad management led his newspaper to be acquired by the Raleigh *Observer*, which later became the *News & Observer*. Under the fiery editorship of Josephus Daniels, it continued the Turner tradition as mouthpiece for white-supremacist Democrats. Turner ran several times for office but only succeeded in winning a state House term in 1878.

John G. Lea continued in the tobacco business in Caswell County, outliving all his accomplices in the Stephens murder and keeping their secrets until his "Confession," given in 1919 upon request of the state historical commission on condition it be sealed until his death, was published in 1935. Lea was ninety-two when he died.

As for Chicken Stephens, his family left Caswell County after the murder. However, the Methodists who rejected Stephens in life received him back in death. His body lies in the church cemetery in Yanceyville, toward a back corner well away from the street. His gravestone reads "John Walter Stephens/Soldier—C.S.A.—patriot."

Whatever were they thinking?

NOTES

May 21, 1870

1. This account of John Walter Stephens's final hours is based on multiple sources: Stedman, *Life and Death of John W. Stephens*, 19–33; Carlton, "Assassination of John Walter Stephens," 1–12; McIver, "Murder of a Scalawag," 12–18. *Hillsborough Recorder*, May 25, June 1, 1870; John G. Lea, "Confession," account of the Stephens killing and other activity by the author during Reconstruction, North Carolina Historical Commission, 1919, http://www.rootsweb.ancestry.com/~nccaswel/misc/confession.htm (accessed February 22, 2009); Trelease, *White Terror*, 212–13.
2. Stedman, *Life and Death of John W. Stephens*, 34.
3. Harris, *William Woods Holden*, 48.
4. Raper, *William W. Holden*, 105.
5. Trelease, *White Terror*, 213.
6. Powell, *When the Past Refused to Die*, 239–42; Lea, "Confession"; Stedman, *Life and Death of John W. Stephens*, 27.

Ominous Victory

7. A Texas cavalryman named Walsh, loitering behind his retreating unit, fired six shots at Union troops entering the city. He was promptly caught and executed. Barrett, *Sherman's March*, 221–22.
8. U.S. War Department, *Official Records*, 243–44.
9. Simpson and Berlin, *Sherman's Civil War*, 866–67.
10. Sherman, *Memoirs*, 813.
11. Lewis, *Sherman*, 542.
12. Harris, *William Woods Holden*, 123–24.
13. Angley, Cross and Hill, *Sherman's March*, 3–17.
14. Spencer, *Last Ninety Days*, 30.

15. Crooker, Nourse and Brown, *Fifty-Fifth Regiment*, 431.
16. *Raleigh Standard*, April 20, 1865, quoted in Holden, *Memoirs*, 32–33.
17. Foner and Mahoney, *America's Reconstruction*, 76.
18. Perrett, *Ulysses S. Grant*, 363.
19. Quoted in Lewis, *Sherman*, 551–52.
20. Ibid., 552–53.
21. Simpson and Berlin, *Sherman's Civil War*, 867.
22. Sherman, *Memoirs*, xx.
23. Ibid.
24. Barrett, *Sherman's March*, 269–70.
25. Angley, Cross and Hill, *Sherman's March*, 93–96.
26. Ridley, *Army of Tennessee*, 465–66.
27. Simpson and Berlin, *Sherman's Civil War*, 881–82.
28. Ibid., 883–84.

New Regime

29. U.S. War Department, *Official Records*, 462.
30. Holden, *Memoirs*, 34–35.
31. Raper, *William W. Holden*, 49.
32. Arnett, *When Confederate Guns Were Stacked*, 90.
33. Ibid., 482.
34. U.S. War Department, *Official Records*, 462.
35. Ibid.
36. Harris, *William Woods Holden*, 158.
37. Ibid., 159.
38. Holden, *Memoirs*, 54.
39. *Raleigh Standard*, April 20, 1865, quoted in Holden, *Memoirs*, 34–35.
40. U.S. War Department, *Official Records*, 453.
41. Ridley, *Army of Tennessee*, 466–69.
42. Anderson, *Piedmont Plantation*, 117.
43. Spencer, *Last Ninety Days*, 43.
44. Ibid., 261–62.
45. Harris, *William Woods Holden*, 163.
46. Raper, *William W. Holden*, 61; Holden, *Memoirs*, 47.
47. *New York Times*, May 30, 1865.
48. Blue, *Salmon P. Chase*, 249–51.
49. Harris, *William Woods Holden*, 166.
50. Holden, *Memoirs*, 57–58.
51. Ibid., 165.
52. Hamilton, *Reconstruction in North Carolina*; Harris, *William Woods Holden*, 165–68, 171; Raper, *William W. Holden*, 64–66.
53. Holden, *Memoirs*, 57–58.
54. Hamilton, *Reconstruction in North Carolina*, 108–9.

55. Harris, *William Woods Holden*, 172.
56. Holden to Andrew Johnson, August 26, 1865, quoted in Harris, *William Woods Holden*, 70.
57. Harris, *William Woods Holden*, 183; Holden, *Memoirs*, 60–61; Raper, *William W. Holden*, 69.

ISSUES BLACK AND WHITE

58. Blue, *Salmon P. Chase*, 248–54.
59. Scott Reynolds Nelson, "Red Strings and Half Brothers," in Inscoe and Kenzer, *Enemies of the Country*, 43.
60. Harris, *William Woods Holden*, 150–51.
61. Raper, *William W. Holden*, 71.
62. Blue, *Salmon P. Chase*, 254.
63. Holden, *Memoirs*, 50–51.
64. Foner and Mahoney, *America's Reconstruction*, 37.
65. Murray, *Proud Shoes*, 170.
66. Raper, *William W. Holden*, 71–72.
67. Quoted in Powell, *When the Past Refused to Die*, 228.
68. Quoted in Medley, *We As Freemen*, 54.
69. Elliott, *Color-Blind Justice*, 99.
70. Medley, *We As Freemen*, 57.
71. Elliott, *Color-Blind Justice*, 103–6.
72. Winston, *It's a Far Cry*, 26.
73. Harris, *William Woods Holden*, 186.
74. Hamilton, *Reconstruction in North Carolina*, 63–68; Harris, *William Woods Holden*, 185–91; Raper, *William W. Holden*, 73–79.
75. Holden, *Memoirs*, 65–66.
76. Harris, *William Woods Holden*, 194.
77. *Daily Standard*, November 29, 1865.
78. Hamilton, *Reconstruction in North Carolina*, 68–69; Harris, *William Woods Holden*, 197–99; Raper, *William W. Holden*, 83–85.

THE MAN WHO WOULD BE GOVERNOR

79. Holden, *Memoirs*, 95.
80. Raper, "William Woods Holden," 169–71.
81. *Official Letters of Alexander Spotswood*, 71.
82. Byrd, *History of the Dividing Line*, 27.
83. Powell, *When the Past Refused to Die*, 20.
84. Anderson, *Durham County*, 23–24.
85. Folk and Shaw, *William Woods Holden*, 6–7; Raper, *William W. Holden*, 3.
86. Folk and Shaw, *William Woods Holden*, 8–11; Harris, *William Woods Holden*, 8–11; Raper, *William W. Holden*, 4–8.

87. White, *Southern Presbyterian Leaders*, 205.
88. Holden, *Memoirs*, 150 n. 1.
89. Ibid., 94.
90. Ibid., 96.
91. *Recorder*, October 28, 1840.
92. Harris, *William Woods Holden*, 12–13; Raper, *William W. Holden*, 9–11.
93. Holden, *Memoirs*, 97.
94. Harris, *William Woods Holden*, 13–81; Raper, *William W. Holden*, 9–33.

BRIGHT LEAVES AND IMPENDING CRISIS

95. Kenzer, *Kinship and Neighborhood*.
96. Troxler and Vincent, *Shuttle & Plow*, 178–82; Anderson, *Durham County*, 61.
97. Olmsted, *Seaboard Slave States*, 348–50.
98. A portion of the Bennitt farm, including the restored cabin and outbuildings, is a North Carolina State Historic Site in Durham. See www.nchistoricsites.org/Bennett/Bennett.htm.
99. Powell, *When the Past Refused to Die*, 168.
100. Ibid., 110; Anderson, *Durham County*, 55, 94; Troxler and Vincent, *Shuttle & Plow*, 222.
101. Powell, *When the Past Refused to Die*, 100.
102. Caswell County Historical Association, "Historical Sketch," www.rootsweb.ancestry.com/~ncccha/memoranda/caswellcounty.html.
103. Ibid.
104. Powell, *When the Past Refused to Die*, 158–61.
105. Ibid., 144.
106. Troxler and Vincent, *Shuttle & Plow*, 226.
107. Tilley, *Bright Tobacco Industry*, 23.
108. Troxler and Vincent, *Shuttle & Plow*, 183; Ready, *Tar Heel State*, 183; Escott, *Many Excellent People*, 178.
109. Cecil-Fronsman, *Common Whites*, 125.
110. Communication Solutions, "North Carolina Business History," www.historync.org (accessed September 12, 2009).
111. Henry David Thoreau, *Walden* (Boston: Houghton Mifflin Co. Riverside Editions, 1960), 81–82.
112. Powell, *When the Past Refused to Die*, 179.
113. *North Carolina Standard*, October 26, November 2 and 30, 1859.
114. Harris, *William Woods Holden*, 84–85.
115. *Standard*, March 14, 1860; Harris, *William Woods Holden*, 84–87.
116. *Standard*, June 11, 1860.
117. Harris, *William Woods Holden*, 82–106; Raper, *William W. Holden*, 33–40.

THE BLACK REPUBLICAN

118. *Standard*, March 6, 1866.
119. Raper, *William W. Holden*, 89.
120. Harris, *William Woods Holden*, says there were nine counties represented, 107. Raper, *William W. Holden*, says thirteen, 88.
121. Harris, *William Woods Holden*, 207; *Standard*, September 26, 1866.
122. *New York Times*, January 20, 1866.
123. Winston, *It's a Far Cry*, 26–27.
124. Hamilton, *History of North Carolina*, 74–76.
125. Ready, *Tar Heel State*, 252.
126. Raper, *William W. Holden*, 89.
127. Harris, *William Woods Holden*, 108–9.
128. *Troy* [New York] *Daily News*, February 18, 1867, quoted in Raper, *William W. Holden*, 90.
129. Campbell, *When Sherman Marched*, 100.
130. *New York Times*, January 14, 1867.
131. April 25, May 9, 1865, in the Elizabeth Collier Diary, #1335-z, Southern Historical Collection, Wilson Library, University of North Carolina at Chapel Hill.
132. Chamberlain, *Old Days in Chapel Hill*, 87.
133. Ibid., 117, 125; Webb, *Jule Carr*, 26.
134. Ready, *Tar Heel State*, 253.
135. "Freedmen's Bureau Report of Outrages in North Carolina, June 1866–January 1867," Freedmen's Bureau Online, www.freedmensbureau.com/northcarolina/ncarolinaoutrages.htm (accessed October 4, 2009).
136. *Minutes of the Freedmen's Convention*, 7–27.
137. Harris, *William Woods Holden*, 210–13; Raper, *William W. Holden*, 90.

SCALAWAG AND CARPETBAGGER

138. Elliott, *Color-Blind Justice*, 107–8.
139. Hamilton, *Reconstruction in North Carolina*, 165.
140. Lea, "Confession."
141. Harris, *William Woods Holden*, 212–17; Raper, *William W. Holden*, 90–91.
142. Zuber, *North Carolina During Reconstruction*, 10–12; Raper, *William W. Holden*, 96–97, 122.
143. Harris, *William Woods Holden*, 214–15; Raper, *William W. Holden*, 94.
144. Nelson, "Red Strings," 37–42; Troxler and Vincent, *Shuttle & Plow*, 295–300.
145. Harris, *William Woods Holden*, 227–29; Raper, *William W. Holden*, 95–97.
146. Powell, *North Carolina*, 388.
147. Hamilton, *Reconstruction in North Carolina*, 222, 226; Harris, *William Woods Holden*, 230–31; Powell, *North Carolina*, 392.

148. Hamilton, *History of North Carolina*, 102.
149. Harris, *William Woods Holden*, 233; Elliott, *Color-Blind Justice*, 112–19.
150. Powell, *North Carolina*, 393.
151. Hamilton, *History of North Carolina*, 111.
152. Ibid., 106.
153. Hamilton, *Reconstruction in North Carolina*, 231; Harris, *William Woods Holden*, 237.
154. Harris, *William Woods Holden*, 239; Elliott, *Color-Blind Justice*, 121.
155. Hamilton, *Reconstruction in North Carolina*, 257.
156. Raper, *William W. Holden*, 156.
157. David Schenck, Diary, April 12, 1868, quoted in Bradley David Proctor, "The Reconstruction of White Supremacy: The Ku Klux Klan in Piedmont North Carolina, 1868 to 1872" (master's thesis, University of North Carolina at Chapel Hill, 2009), 10.
158. Holden, *Memoirs*, 101–2.
159. Elliott, *Color-Blind Justice*, 132.
160. Ibid., 136; Stedman, *Life and Death of John W. Stephens*, 18.
161. Stedman, *Life and Death of John W. Stephens*, 6.
162. Carlton, "Assassination of John Walter Stephens," 1.
163. Stedman, *Life and Death of John W. Stephens*, 6.
164. Allen W. Trelease, "John Walter Stephens," in Powell, ed., *Dictionary of North Carolina Biography*, 439.
165. Carlton, "Assassination of John Walter Stephens," 2–4; Stedman, *Life and Death of John W. Stephens*, 8–15; Trelease, "Stephens," 440.

Corruption and Ku Klux

166. Harris, *William Woods Holden*, 243–44; Raper, *William W. Holden*, 102.
167. Holden, *Memoirs*, 108–12
168. Harris, *William Woods Holden*, 245, 255–63.
169. Eleanor Swain to Cornelia Phillips Spencer, Cornelia Phillips Spencer Papers (#683), Southern Historical Collection, University of North Carolina at Chapel Hill.
170. Chamberlain, *Old Days in Chapel Hill*, 99; Webb, *Jule Carr*, 25.
171. Harris, *William Woods Holden*, 264–66.
172. Webb, *Jule Carr*, 28–29.
173. Hamilton, *History of North Carolina*, 105.
174. Harris, *William Woods Holden*, 249.
175. Hamilton, *History of North Carolina*, 116–17.
176. Holden, *Memoirs*, 115–18.
177. J.W. Stephens to W.W. Holden, quoted in Trelease, *White Terror*, 212–13.
178. Stedman, *Life and Death of John W. Stephens*, 36.
179. Raper, *William W. Holden*, 127–28.
180. Harris, *William Woods Holden*, 269–70; Foner, *Reconstruction*, 166; "Augustus Summerfield Merrimon," www.heritagewnc.org/people/merrimon_augustus_summerfield.htm (accessed October 18, 2009).

181. Caswell County Historical Association, "George William Swepson (1819–1883)," http://nccha.blogspot.com/2006/11/george-william-swepson-1819-1883.html (accessed October 18, 2009).
182. Harris, *William Woods Holden*, 273–74.
183. Raper, *William W. Holden*, 129–39.
184. Harris, *William Woods Holden*, 276–77.
185. Troxler and Vincent, *Shuttle & Plow*, 326–27.
186. Nelson, "Red Strings," 45–46.
187. Holden, *Memoirs*, 136–37; Raper, *William W. Holden*, 159.
188. Raper, *William W. Holden*, 161.

THE KU KLUX EXPERIENCE

189. Holden, *Memoirs*, 136.
190. Holden to Belknap, November 16, 1869, quoted in Harris, *William Woods Holden*, 282.
191. U.S. Congress, *Report on the alleged outrages*, 19.
192. Proctor, "White Supremacy," 10.
193. Anderson, *Durham County*, 103; *Durham Morning Herald*, "Local Veterans Played Part in Original Klan," March 10, 1929.
194. "Local Veterans."
195. U.S. Congress, *Report on the alleged outrages*, 17–20.
196. Albion Tourgee to William Holden, July 3, 1869, quoted in Raper, *William W. Holden*, 160.
197. Troxler and Vincent, *Shuttle & Plow*, 327–28.
198. Holden, *Memoirs*, 138–39.
199. Raper, *William W. Holden*, 163.
200. *Recorder*, January 26, 1870.
201. Ibid.
202. Harris, *William Woods Holden*, 281.
203. Holden, *Memoirs*, 79.
204. Ibid., 123.
205. Trelease, *White Terror*, 211.
206. U.S. Congress, *Report on the alleged outrages*, 18.
207. Trelease, *White Terror*, 210.
208. Paul Hambrick to William Holden, March 12, 1870, quoted in Raper, *William W. Holden*, 174.
209. Cecil-Fronsman, *Common Whites*, 218.
210. William Holden to U.S. Grant, March 10, 1868, quoted in Raper, *William W. Holden*, 164.
211. Harris, *William Woods Holden*, 285.
212. *Recorder*, May 18, 1870.
213. North Carolina, General Assembly Senate, *The Trial of William W. Holden, Governor of North Carolina, on Impeachment by the House of Representatives for High Crimes and Misdemeanors* (Raleigh, NC: Sentinel Printing, 1871), 1146.

214. *Recorder*, May 18, 1870.
215. Manarin, *North Carolina Troops*, 202; Lea, "Confession," 1; Powell, *When the Past Refused to Die*, 235–36.
216. John W. Stephens to William Holden, May 16, 1870, quoted in Troxler and Vincent, *Shuttle & Plow*, 330.
217. Lea, "Confession," 2.

A War, of Sorts

218. *Recorder*, June 1, 1870.
219. Raper, *William W. Holden*, 166.
220. Stedman, *Life and Death of John W. Stephens*, 39; *Recorder*, June 29, 1870.
221. Albion W. Tourgee to Joseph C. Abbott, May 24, 1870, http://www.digitalhistory.uh.edu/reconstruction/section4/section4_tourgeekkk.htm (accessed August 17, 2009).
222. Harris, *William Woods Holden*, 188. Raper, *William W. Holden*, 167–69.
223. Raper, *William W. Holden*, 167–69.
224. Timothy M. Osment, "Kirk's Raiders," Mountain Heritage Center and Western Carolina University, 2008, http://www.digitalheritage.org/index.php/heritage-moments/heritage-moment-essays/21-kirks-raiders (accessed October 20, 2009).
225. *Salisbury* [North Carolina] *Daily Watchman*, June 30, 1864.
226. *Recorder*, June 29, 1870.
227. U.S. Congress, *Report on the alleged outrages*, 11–12; Harris, *William Woods Holden*, 289; Raper, *William W. Holden*, 170–71; Trelease, *White Terror*, 216–17.
228. Powell, *When the Past Refused to Die*, 244–47.
229. Lea, "Confession," 5.
230. Folk and Shaw, *William Woods Holden*, 216–18; Harris, *William Woods Holden*, 193–96; Raper, *William W. Holden*, 176–82.
231. William Holden to Richmond Pearson, July 19, 1870, quoted in Raper, *William W. Holden*, 177.
232. Harris, *William Woods Holden*, 298; Raper, *William W. Holden*, 186–87; Zuber, *North Carolina During Reconstruction*, 41.
233. *Sentinel*, August 3, 1870, quoted in Folk and Shaw, *William Woods Holden*, 220–21.
234. *New York Times*, September 4, 1870.

Reprisals and Redemptions

235. Harris, *William Woods Holden*, 299–300; Raper, *William W. Holden*, 199–200.
236. *Standard*, October 11, 1870.
237. Harris, *William Woods Holden*, 305.
238. Holden, *Memoirs*, 147.
239. George Swepson to A.J. Jones, February 12, 1871, quoted in Raper, *William W. Holden*, 213.

240. Harris, *William Woods Holden*, 305–9; Raper, *William W. Holden*, 211–21.
241. Raper, *William W. Holden*, 251.
242. Harris, *William Woods Holden*, 313–17; Raper, *William W. Holden*, 233–51.
243. Hamilton, *History of North Carolina*, 127; Turner, *Florida Railroads*, 41–44.

BIBLIOGRAPHY

Anderson, Jean Bradley. *Durham County.* Durham, NC: Duke University Press and Historic Preservation Society of Durham, 1990.

———. *Piedmont Plantation: The Bennehan-Cameron Family and Lands in North Carolina.* Durham, NC: Historic Preservation Society of Durham, 1985.

Angley, Wilson, Jerry L. Cross and Michael Hill. *Sherman's March Through North Carolina: A Chronology.* Raleigh: North Carolina Division of Archives and History, 1995.

Arnett, Ethel Stephens. *When Confederate Guns Were Stacked, Greensboro, North Carolina.* Greensboro, NC: Piedmont Press, 1965.

Barrett, John G. *Sherman's March Through the Carolinas.* Chapel Hill: University of North Carolina Press, 1956.

Blue, Frederic J. *Salmon P. Chase: A Life in Politics.* Kent, OH: Kent State University Press, 1987.

Byrd, William. *History of the Dividing Line.* Petersburg, VA: Edmund and Julian C. Ruffin, 1841.

Campbell, Jacqueline Glass. *When Sherman Marched North From the Sea: Resistance on the Confederate Home Front.* Chapel Hill and London: University of North Carolina Press, 2003.

Carlton, Luther M. "Assassination of John Walter Stephens." In *Legal and Biographical Studies Published by the Historical Society of Trinity College.* Series II. N.p., 1898.

Cecil-Fronsman, Bill. *Common Whites: Class and Culture in Antebellum North Carolina.* Lexington: University Press of Kentucky, 1992.

Chamberlain, Hope Summerell. *Old Days in Chapel Hill: Being the Life and Letters of Cornelia Phillips Spencer.* Chapel Hill and London: University of North Carolina Press, 1926.

Crooker, Lucien B., Henry Stedman Nourse and John G. Brown. *The Story of the Fifty-Fifth Regiment Illinois Volunteer Infantry in the Civil War 1861–1865 by a Committee of the Regiment.* Clinton, MA: W.J. Coulter, 1887.

Elliott, Mark Emory. *Color-Blind Justice: Albion Tourgee and the Quest for Racial Equality.* New York and Cary, NC: Oxford University Press, 2006.

Escott, Paul D. *Many Excellent People: Power and Privilege in North Carolina, 1850–1890.* Chapel Hill and London: University of North Carolina Press, 1985.

Folk, Edgar E., and Bynum Shaw. *William Woods Holden: A Political Biography.* Winston-Salem, NC: John F. Blair, 1982.

Foner, Eric. *A Short History of Reconstruction, 1863–77.* New York: Harper & Row, 1990.

Foner, Eric, and Olivia Mahoney. *America's Reconstruction.* New York: HarperPerennial, 1995.

Hamilton, Joseph Gregoire de Roulhac. *History of North Carolina: Volume III, North Carolina Since 1860.* Chicago and New York: Lewis Publishing, 1919.

———. *Reconstruction in North Carolina.* New York: Columbia University Press, 1914.

Harris, William C. *William Woods Holden: Firebrand of North Carolina Politics.* Baton Rouge and London: Louisiana State University Press, 1987.

Holden, William Woods. *Memoirs of W.W. Holden.* Vol. 2. Durham, NC: Trinity College Historical Society, 1911.

Inscoe, John C., and Robert C. Kenzer. *Enemies of the Country: New Perspectives on Unionists in the Civil War South.* Athens: University of Georgia Press, 2001.

Kenzer, Robert C. *Kinship and Neighborhood in a Southern Community: Orange County, North Carolina, 1849–1861.* Knoxville: University of Tennessee Press, 1987.

Lewis, Lloyd. *Sherman: Fighting Prophet.* New York: Harcourt, Brace and Company, 1932.

Manarin, Louis H. *North Carolina Troops 1861–1865: A Roster.* Vol. 2. Raleigh: North Carolina Division of Archives and History, 1966.

McIver, Stuart. "The Murder of a Scalawag." *American History Illustrated*, April 1973.

Medley, Keith Weldon. *We As Freemen: Plessy v. Ferguson.* Gretna, LA: Pelican, 2003.

Minutes of the Freedmen's Convention, Held in the City of Raleigh, On the 2nd, 3rd, 4th and 5th of October, 1866. Raleigh, NC: Standard Book and Job Office, 1866.

Murray, Pauli. *Proud Shoes: The Story of an American Family.* Boston: Beacon Press, 1956.

North Carolina. *Proclamations by the Governor of North Carolina, Together With the Opinion of Chief-Justice Pearson and the Reply of the Governor.* Raleigh, NC: Standard Steam Book and Job Print, 1870.

The Official Letters of Alexander Spotswood, Lieutenant-Governor of the Colony of Virginia 1710–1722. Richmond: Virginia Historical Society, 1882.

Olmsted, Frederick Law. *A Journey in the Seaboard Slave States.* New York: Dix and Edwards, 1856.

Perrett, Geoffrey. *Ulysses S. Grant: Soldier & President.* New York: Random House, 1997.

Powell, William F. *When the Past Refused to Die: A History of Caswell County 1777–1977.* Yanceyville, NC: Caswell County Historical Association, 1977.

Powell, William S., ed. *Dictionary of North Carolina Biography.* Vol. 5. Chapel Hill and London: University of North Carolina Press, 1994.

———. *North Carolina Through Four Centuries.* Chapel Hill and London: University of North Carolina Press, 1989.

Raper, Horace W. *William W. Holden: North Carolina's Political Enigma.* Chapel Hill and London: University of North Carolina Press, 1985.

———. "William Woods Holden." In *Dictionary of North Carolina Biography*, edited by William S. Powell, vol. 3. Chapel Hill: University of North Carolina Press, 1979–1996.

Ready, Milton. *The Tar Heel State: A History of North Carolina.* Columbia: University of South Carolina Press, 2005.

Ridley, Bromfield Lewis. *Battles and Sketches of the Army of Tennessee.* Mexico: Missouri Printing, 1906.

Sherman, William T. *Memoirs of General W.T. Sherman.* New York: Library of America, 1990.

Simpson, Brooks D., and Jean V. Berlin, eds. *Sherman's Civil War: Selected Correspondence of William T. Sherman.* Chapel Hill and London: University of North Carolina Press, 1999.

Spencer, Cornelia Phillips. *The Last Ninety Days of the War in North-Carolina.* New York: Watchman Publishing Company, 1866.

Stedman, Andrew J. *History of the Life and Death of John W. Stephens, State Senator of North Carolina, From Caswell County.* Greensboro, NC: Patriot Print, 1870.

Tilley, Nannie Mae. *The Bright Tobacco Industry 1860–1929.* Chapel Hill: University of North Carolina Press, 1948.

Trelease, Allen W. *White Terror: The Ku Klux Klan Conspiracy and Southern Reconstruction.* New York: Harper & Row, 1971.

Troxler, Carole Watterson, and William Murray Vincent. *Shuttle & Plow: A History of Alamance County, North Carolina.* Graham, NC: Alamance County Historical Association, 1999.

Turner, Gregg. *A Short History of Florida Railroads.* Charleston, SC: Arcadia Publishing, 2003.

U.S. Congress, Senate, Select Committee of the [U.S.] Senate. *Report on the alleged outrages in the Southern states by the select committee of the senate.* 42nd Congress, 1st session, Senate, Report 1.

U.S. War Department, U.S. Records and Pensions Office, U.S. War Records Office et al. *The War of the Rebellion: A Compilation of the Official Records of the Union and Confederate Armies.* Series I, vol. XLVII, part III. Washington, D.C.: Government Printing Office, 1895.

Webb, Mena. *Jule Carr: General Without an Army.* Chapel Hill and London: University of North Carolina Press, 1987.

White, Henry Alexander. *Southern Presbyterian Leaders.* New York: Neale Publishing Co., 1911.

Winston, Robert Watson. *It's a Far Cry.* Spartanburg, SC: Reprint Company, Publishers, 2001.

Zuber, Richard L. *North Carolina During Reconstruction.* Raleigh: North Carolina Division of Archives and History, 1969.

ABOUT THE AUTHOR

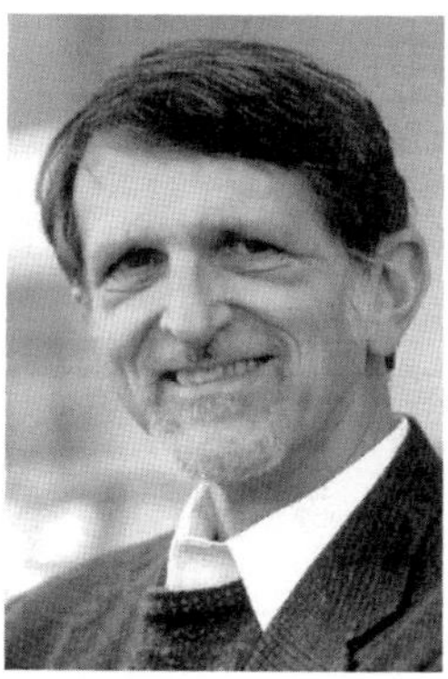

Harry Lynch photo, courtesy the News & Observer.

Born in Georgia, raised in Florida and resident of North Carolina since 1966, Jim Wise is an alumnus of Duke University (BA, English) and the University of North Carolina (MA, folklore). He has been a reporter, editor and/or columnist for newspapers in Durham, North Carolina, for more than twenty-eight years and has taught adult classes on local and Southern history for the Osher Lifelong Learning Institute at Duke. His previous History Press books are *On Sherman's Trail: The Civil War's North Carolina Climax* and *Durham Tales: The Morris Street Maple, the Plastic Cow, the Durham Day that Was and More*. He and his wife, Babs, live in Durham with an aging dog and cat.